KEEPING QUIET

KEEPING QUIET

Sixteen Essays on Silence

ADRIANA PÁRAMO

🐓 Red Hen Press | *Pasadena, CA*

Book design by Mark E. Cull.

Library of Congress Cataloging-in-Publication Data

Names: Páramo, Adriana, 1966– author.
Title: Keeping quiet: sixteen essays on silence / Adriana Páramo.
Description: First edition. | Pasadena, CA: Red Hen Press, 2024.
Identifiers: LCCN 2024006051 (print) | LCCN 2024006052 (ebook) | ISBN 9781636281841 (paperback) | ISBN 9781636281858 (ebook)
Subjects: LCGFT: Essays.
Classification: LCC PR9312.9.P37 K44 2024 (print) | LCC PR9312.9.P37 (ebook) | DDC 302.2—dc23/eng/20240304
LC record available at https://lccn.loc.gov/2024006051
LC ebook record available at https://lccn.loc.gov/2024006052

Publication of this book has been made possible in part through the generous financial support of Ann Beman.

The National Endowment for the Arts, the Los Angeles County Arts Commission, the Ahmanson Foundation, the Dwight Stuart Youth Fund, the Max Factor Family Foundation, the Pasadena Tournament of Roses Foundation, the Pasadena Arts & Culture Commission and the City of Pasadena Cultural Affairs Division, the City of Los Angeles Department of Cultural Affairs, the Audrey & Sydney Irmas Charitable Foundation, the Meta & George Rosenberg Foundation, the Albert and Elaine Borchard Foundation, the Adams Family Foundation, Amazon Literary Partnership, the Sam Francis Foundation, and the Mara W. Breech Foundation partially support Red Hen Press.

First Edition
Published by Red Hen Press
www.redhen.org

Acknowledgments

Portions of this manuscript have appeared under different titles and in different incarnations as follows:

The Masters Review: "An Arab Man and an English Woman Walk Into a Bar"; *New Millennium Writings*: "Teaching Mom Long Division"; *Solstice Literary Magazine*: "Milk, Oil, and a Night of Tequila," "A Minute of Silence"; *Southern Indiana Review*: "Love on the Iditarod Road"; *WOW, Women on Writing*: "Dear Julie."

To all who remained quiet. This book is dedicated to you.

For your muffled screams

Your well-kept secrets

Your bruises, fears, and shame

This book honors your silent strength.

Contents

To write is also not to speak. It is to keep silent.
It is to howl noiselessly. —Marguerite Duras

1

A Minute of Silence

I'm lying on my back, scrawny feet up in the stirrups. In my head, I go like, Don't look, don't look, don't you look at her, but of course, I do. I raise my head, and there next to the gynecologist is mom, peering into my most private me. Mom cranes her neck over the doctor's head to bear witness, to be there when the doctor announces her verdict.

So, okay, last night I broke my 6:00 p.m. curfew. My mom thinks that the world is hunky-dory until 5:59 p.m., at which point evil crawls out of his lair (evil is a man) and makes men crazy and women weak. It wasn't entirely my fault that I didn't make it home on time. I blame it on Diego, my boyfriend. Well, he is not my boyfriend; he couldn't be, because Diego is a blond, super hot, surfer-looking, fifteen-year-old papito who plays the guitar and has what he calls "a few miles under his hood." He is the type of boy who could have any girl in the neighborhood and its surroundings, so naturally, when he asked me, a thirteen-year-old brown, flat-chested, homely looking girl, to go for a spin, I nearly died. I know I'm not a looker, and when a girl wants a boy who is way out of her league, she has to give him something he wants. It's common knowledge in school. Hello? Anyway, last night, we rode our bikes behind the stadium, where the grass is tall and the streetlights dim. I put into practice everything I had read in Cosmopolitan: I licked my lips a lot. I mean, I licked them so far that my upper lip started to hurt, okay? I had what Cosmopolitan called a willing mouth, wore a blouse with buttons that responded to the slightest touch, and a training bra that offered zero resistance to his curious hands. Except he was not interested in what I had to offer. Instead, we parked our bikes, took the guitar out of its case, sang "Hotel California" in botched English, then rolled a joint. I wanted to try it, but mom is like a hound dog; she can smell alcohol, cigarettes, boys, lies, dreams, the tangible, and the intangible. I thought, Yes, Please, but said, No, Thank you, fully knowing I had blown my chance with him now that he knew I was nothing but a little girl afraid of upsetting her mommy. Someone shoot me. I lay on the grass, buttoned up my plaid shirt, which I had worn just for the occasion, and stared at the darkening sky. Then Diego started to mumble some nonsense about, like, politics, maybe? I don't know, and between his tedious ramblings, my disappointment, and the smell of his joint, I fell asleep. Sayonara. When I woke up, Diego was strapping his guitar case across his chest while humming more "Hotel California." I can tell you this: there was no cool wind in my hair or soft smell of colitas rising up through the air. Just the conviction that my mom could very well carry out her legendary threat of turning my piehole upside down for disobeying her.

The gynecologist doesn't address me. I am a pocket of air. In her office, only she and mom exist. I am a piece of meat on a slab. She rubs her hands together, and I wonder if it is out of anticipation for what she is about to discover, a Let's-see-what-we've-got-here type of keenness, or to warm up her hands before slipping them into a pair of latex gloves. She clears her throat. I'm tearing up from the crushing weight of the humiliation. I look at mom with pleading eyes, but she is more interested in that spot between my legs. In my head, I go, Tell her to leave, ask her to leave, beg her to leave, mami por favor. I think, Close your legs, do not, under any circumstances, let her look at you down there. But mom is the customer in this establishment, and the customer is always right. Mom places her hand on the doctor's shoulder, the doctor pats mom's fingers. Do they know each other? Mom is borderline illiterate; she doesn't have educated friends. Wait, maybe they are not friends at all, and what I'm witnessing here is a mother-to-mother moment of mutual understanding. I have mistaken this primal, tribal, stupid, ignorant, ill-founded exchange of signals for friendship. The doctor turns her face sideways and whispers something in mom's direction. It must be important because mom lowers her right ear to hear the doctor's words. Mom nods. Whatever the doctor says, mom agrees with her. I'm here, I want to say. I'm here. Why are you doing this to me? Even better, what exactly are you doing to me? The doctor doesn't ask me how I am or bother to explain what she is about to do. I am one of the dummies she practiced resuscitation on in medical school. She raises her gloved right hand and flexes her fingers. She wants to unfold me; she wants my body to tell her gloved fingers something critical, something that will change my mom's life, I think, I don't know, maybe even mine.

What was I saying? Oh yeah, let me tell you about last night. On my way home from the stadium, I knew my mom was going to kill me. And here's the funny thing. Mom has never hit me. Not once. But maybe because I was the last of six children and the closest sister is six years older than me, I grew up pretty much like an only child surrounded by older siblings and an overbearing mom. I experience mom's wrath as a harbinger of the world's end. No, she doesn't hit me, never has; instead, she punishes me with her silence, which is the meanest emotional punishment ever, for all intents and purposes. I know that when the queen doesn't address her citizens and servants, they might as well throw themselves off a cliff. Sometimes I think mom is afraid of me growing up. If I do, there will be no more motherly responsibilities left for her, and without her role as a mother, she is, honestly, nothing. That's why she clings to me; oh, man, when I think of mom's grip on me, the only word that comes to mind is *barnacle*. I can't cut my hair, shave my legs, or choose my own goddamn clothes. Mom owns me, defines me. I am because she is. She is my alpha and my omega. If I anger her, I cease to exist for days, weeks, months. I can't bear her silent wrath. And because I feel that my life depends on her recognition of mine, I made up a big fat lie. I wanted magically to transform her anger into empathy, her fury into something in the vicinity of tenderness.

I was kidnapped by a group of men who dragged me from the street and threw me into their car. What? Where did they take me? Er, I dunno. I passed out—they must have drugged me or something—and that's why I lost track of time and broke my curfew. There. I said it. My sisters rolled their eyes, bored with the ridiculousness of my newest lie. Pfft. Mom simply stared at me. I mean, she didn't just look at me; she flew through me, turned me inside out, held my heart in her hands, and watched it beat. If she doubted me, was worried, appalled, or disgusted, she didn't show it. If my trick had worked and she felt empathy, she didn't show it either. While she appeared calm, which was a very good thing, I knew I was a single gesture away from being hauled into her silent hell. Mom just locked her eyes on mine, the way she looks at the cutting board when she is chopping onions, utterly enthralled by the seesaw motion of her fingers, like she doesn't want to miss a thing, then she smoothed her apron over her skirt, stood up, slowly, methodically, and sent me to bed. I had escaped mom's pre-apocalyptic fury.

I couldn't believe my own cunning.

Boo-yah.

This morning, after my siblings had gone to work and school, mom instructed me to shower and get dressed. We had a doctor's appointment, she announced. She was steely. Not angry angry, but, you know, her voice had a bit of vinegar and a bit of salt, like she was making salad dressing every time she spoke to me. When she is like this, I lose my bearings and become so unsure of myself that I forget simple things like walking in a straight line or how to brush my teeth. I grow clumsy, spill things, and trip on my own shoes. I am unsteady and lopsided in her soundless shadow and move around her as if I'm walking on broken glass, ready to cut myself and bleed to death at any moment. Naturally, I didn't have the guts to ask her which doctor's appointment she was talking about. I wasn't ill; I certainly didn't need a doctor; therefore, it had to be for her. Her lower back always hurts, especially when we disobey her. My sister says that mom somatizes all her problems, whatever that means.

My body refuses to open its door for the doctor. My oval closes in, and its vertexes clench to one another, resisting the two prodding fingers. It hurts, but I don't make a peep because my mom doesn't like crybabies. I know I have a job: to melt into the table silently, to be the good girl I wasn't last evening, and to do as I'm told. No one knows I'm here. Right now, I don't exist outside these four walls. I am not a sister, not a friend, not a cousin, not a student, not a neighbor. I am nobody's girlfriend. I'm not the bookworm that uses big words and argues with everyone—except mom, of course. I'm just a thirteen-year-old specimen under inspection. I don't know that I can shout, that I can howl. I don't know I have the right to close my legs, pull up my panties, and walk out of the office. I don't know that I have rights. No one has ever talked to me about my body, not even my mom. The first time I bled, mom asked me to pull down my panties in front of her and show her the stain. Satisfied with the sight, she gave me a sanitary napkin, showed me how to use it, and kissed me on my forehead. Congratulations, she said, you are a woman now. That it? I thought. Now what?

I fixate my eyes on the second hand of a wall clock to my right. I count every tick. Uno, dos, tres. The doctor's fingers prod and prod, but they can't make it past the pearly gates, which seems to annoy her. She sighs dramatically and turns her chair 180 degrees; mom moves out of her way momentarily, phew, the doctor reaches into a cabinet and gets a tube of something she opens with her teeth. Doce, trece, catorce. Mom repositions herself. Fuck me. Veinte, veintiuno, veintidós. The doctor rubs her right fingers with a gelatinous substance, and she pushes them in. I'm split into two. I'm afraid the two halves will never be reunited. Cuarenta y cuatro, cuarenta y cinco, cuarenta y seis. A stream of tears pools in the nest of my ears. The doctor withdraws her fingers, and I'm numb. I try to imagine the scene from above. My dress all bunched up around my waist. My legs spread eagle on the exam table. Mom is right there in the first row, arms across her chest the way she does at the butcher's when she asks him for a nice bone with meat on it, and she takes her do-not-try-to-cheat-me stance, eyes fixated on a femur like a lioness stalking her prey. Suddenly, I'm painfully aware of the coarseness of my pubic hair, the moss on my legs that mom doesn't let me shave, my hairy armpits, the matted frizz of my two braids. No wonder Diego didn't want to touch me. I'm hairy, ugly, and a baby whose body belongs to no one but mom. Cincuenta y nueve. Fifty-nine seconds. A whole minute of silence. Is there anyone in the lobby getting the funeral bugle ready? Will someone play "Taps" as I walk out of here? The day is done, gone the sun.

Mom places her hand on my back and ushers me out of the office. She is pleased. The doctor found what she was looking for. The thing is in mint condition. I'm relieved those *horrible men* didn't harm you, she says. There it is, more vinegar and more salt as she makes a theatrical emphasis on horrible men, revealing that she didn't believe my kidnapping story, but used it anyway to punish me and verify my virginity while at it. Mom rushes down the street. She can't wait to get to the church around the doctor's office. Down there, my panties rub my skin raw. I'm on fire. I'm sore from the intrusion. I want to squat in a pot of luke-warm water until the heat dissipates. Mom takes long strides, but my chafed bits hurt. I can't keep up with her and start falling a few steps behind. That's the way she walks, the way she moves, and imagine the way her mind works: at a racing pace. She never rests, has zero room for idleness, and makes sure we don't either, occupying our weekends with house chores, limiting the time we spend in the shower, and rousing everyone from their sleep early on a Sunday. Clap, clap. Arriba, niñas, arriba. This house won't clean itself.

Mom lights a candle and kneels on the pew. We're thanking God for keeping you safe from harm, mom says. I also light one candle and kneel on the pew beside her, although I don't feel particularly grateful. Mom whispers a heartfelt Holy Father while I stare at the feet of Jesus crucified in front of us. Jesus, the son of a virgin. I want to ask mom if it would have been okay for Joseph to hold Mary down and submit her to a vaginal examination to attest that she was, in fact, a virgin when she announced she was pregnant. Something inside me burns, not just the part rubbing against the fabric of my underwear, but in my belly. Fury, I think. I'm not just pissed off. This must be what fury feels like. I look at Jesus and want to scream. If the cross fell in our direction, which of us two should be crushed under its weight? I make my choice and feel slightly pleased, slightly guilty, but mostly pleased at the thought of a motherless life.

Pray with me, mom commands. I confess to God Almighty, before the whole company of heaven, and to you, my brothers and sisters, that I have sinned in thought, word, and deed; in what I have done and in what I have failed to do, by my fault, by my fault, by my most grievous fault; wherefore I pray God Al-mighty to have mercy on me, forgive me all my sins, and bring me to everlasting life. Amen. I'm about to get up, but mom pulls me back down on my knees and starts the prayer again. Joy of joys. I do as I'm told but can't ignore how mom raises her voice a bit as she says, ". . . that I have sinned in thought, word, and deed; in what I have done and in what I have failed to do . . ." She pauses, looks at me sideways and continues, ". . . by my fault, by my fault, by my most grievous fault . . ." Mom beats her chest lightly with a clenched hand. I stop mumbling the prayer. Mea culpa, mea culpa, my ass. The double whammy of mea culpa mom is forcing out of me is meant to make me feel guilty about some grave sin I committed against God, the Almighty, and mom, his representative on earth. I don't think so.

Later, at home, I open the tome of the encyclopedia corresponding to the letter H. I look up hymen. Hymenaios (Ὑμέναιος), or Hymen, was the god of weddings, specifically the wedding hymn sung by the bride's train as she was escorted to the groom. It is said that Hymenaios had to be present at every wedding, or the ceremony would be disastrous. I look at the Greek art depiction of this God, and I can't believe the hilarity, the irony, the absurdity of it. There he is, a white, winged young boy with a tiny dick carrying a bridal torch somewhere on the bridal train. He looks like a pubescent cupid, unsure of his sexuality. According to the encyclopedia, his superpower is called amokinesis. Yep. Hymenaios had absolute control and divine authority over love, passion, and desire during wedding ceremonies. Hey, I appreciate good imagination and love a good story, but what in the world does this have to do with what happened to me today?

An unwed woman who loses her virginity is damaged goods. No one would ever want to marry her. Every man wants to be the first one. No man likes sloppy seconds. Who wants to be where someone else has been? I have heard mom's list before but never thought it would apply to me too. If being a married woman is to live like mom, I don't want to be married. Ever. I don't want an absent husband who leaves me pregnant every time he comes to visit. I don't want to be poor, and more than anything, I don't want to be uneducated. I don't want to spend my life in the kitchen, mopping floors, and scrubbing clothes. I don't want my youth to pass me by wishing for the love of a man who had no qualms about leaving a wife and six kids to fend for themselves. I don't want mom's stationary life; I want to go far away, to lands she doesn't even know exist. I want mountains other than the Andes, rivers other than the Magdalena, sunsets over distant places that don't resemble Mariquita. I don't want mom's short gray hair; I want mine black and wild, Medusa's snakes coiled about my nape. I don't want mom's rosewood nail polish; I want my fingernails pitch black and bleeding red. I don't want her floral tea-length dresses, her wool cardigans, her lame sense of humor, her old woman's shoes—has mom always been old? I hereby reject her idea that a woman is not whole until she gets married and has children. I refuse to have a man. No, wait, I have a better idea; I'll have many men, many. I'll fling myself into their arms, their beds, their lips, but surrender to none. I look at the stupid image of Hymenaios. Really, Mom, seriously? And I begin to cry hard. I mean, hard like it's freaking pouring down in the Amazon. Biblical type of rain, apocalyptic rain. When mom calls my name, I am a mess of tears, snot, and dribble. Supper is ready.

I don't know if mom told my sisters that she had taken her thirteen-year-old daughter to have a virginity test. No one said anything to me, and I told no one about it. I will always recall that minute of silence on the exam table as the day I lost my innocence. I lost my innocence to you, Mom, while still a virgin. I didn't need to have a man inside me or my hymen ruptured to realize that everything, *everything*, I held dear to my heart, everything that had meaning and power, my dreams, my ambitions, and all the little miraclesI imagined life held in store for me, would be taken away if my hymen was not intact. I lost my innocence the day mom told me without words that the thing between my legs was the whole of me. I was nothing without it. Things like good grades, education, a head screwed on straight, compassion, ethos, and aspirations were all cute things to have, but held no water in the face of a broken hymen.

The memory of that minute in the doctor's office faded with age. I lost my virginity to my daughter's father, divorced him, and married again. I left family and country, traveled the world, lived and worked on different continents. I earned a PhD in something, fell in love, then out of love, loved again, reached middle age, and never ever thought about it until I wrote my first book. In it, I wrote about the incident candidly, humorously, not as an indictment of mom's behavior, but as matter-of-factly as I could afford while mourning her death. Then, the sister closest to me in age contacted me. She had the book translated into Spanish and wanted to say how terribly sorry she had always felt about the kidnapping. It must have been so terrifying. You were so young, she said. I bit into my knuckles. Had the confession of my lie been lost in translation? Did she skip that page? Had she clung to the fantasy of the kidnapping so intensely for so many years that she could no longer see the truth even when spelled out on the page? I didn't know what to say. We locked gazes, her eyes filled with compassion, mine with embarrassment, renewed humiliation, and confusion. After over thirty years, the memory of that minute in the doctor's office hit me full force. I felt naked, spread eagle, scrutinized, again a thirteen-year-old unsure of herself. I had come out clean on the page, but my sister had missed the confession, the apology, the regret. She didn't mention the virginity test, nor did she consider mom's transgression. The kidnapping, those horrible men in the car, such a farfetched lie, I couldn't comprehend why she had believed it all these years. I said that was a long time ago and left it at that.

I grew up hearing the language of virginity, one that reinforces the myth that a woman's body is the most valuable thing she can give to a man and that it's a one-time thing: *She lost her virginity*—Perdió su virginidad; *she gave it up to him*—se lo dió a él; *she was deflowered*—él la desvirgó. Mom's favorite when an unwed woman lost her virginity had a profound connotation of damage: El la perjudicó—*he damaged her.* In times of need—which seemed to be every day of the month—mom used to invoke her army of celestial superheroes: Jesus, Joseph, Mary, souls in purgatory, a cluster of saints—San Gregorio, an uncanonized Venezuelan doctor, being her favorite—and the eleven thousand virgins. Eleven thousand. I chuckle now as I write this because the eleven thousand virgins are a myth, or rather, a mistake made in translation in the late ninth century.

In medieval times, circa 383 AD, a pagan Hun leader invading Cologne shot with an arrow an eleven-year-old British princess named Ursula (*Undecimillia* in Latin) who refused to "give it up to him." Since she was a virgin who allegedly chose death over losing her chastity or renouncing her faith, her death was registered as a martyred virgin. A few centuries later, a monk, most likely a scribe, misread or misinterpreted her Latin name as a number. Where it originally read *Undecimillia* M.V—martyred virgin, he rewrote it as undecimila M.V—eleven thousand martyred virgins.

Oh, Mom.

In the Old Testament, it's written that a new bride should be stoned to death outside of her father's house if her husband claims she was not a virgin on their wedding night and if "no proof of the young woman's virginity can be found." In the Roman Catholic Church, virgins have been consecrated as brides of Christ. While this consecration has been bestowed for centuries only for nuns living in cloistered monasteries, the bestowal for women living in the world was reintroduced under Pope Paul VI in 1970. Estimates derived from the diocesan records oscillate around five thousand consecrated virgins worldwide as of 2018. Five thousand.

Oh, mom.

The Commission on Gender Equality (CGE) and the Human Rights Commission (HRC) have condemned virginity testing worldwide. The testing is seen as humiliating and encroaching on young women's private lives. The World Health Organization defines virginity testing as an examining female genitalia used to determine whether a woman or girl has had vaginal intercourse. The same organization declares that virginity testing has no scientific merit or clinical indication, as the presence of a hymen is not a reliable indication of intercourse, and no known exam can prove a history of vaginal intercourse. *Furthermore, the practice violates the victim's human rights and is associated with both immediate and long-term consequences detrimental to her physical, psychological, and social well-being. The harmful practice of virginity testing is a social, cultural and political issue. Its elimination will require a comprehensive societal response supported by the public health community and health professionals.*

In the nineties in South Africa, the testing was viewed as an effort to handle the AIDS epidemic, albeit by exerting greater control over women and their sexuality. However, in June 2005, the South African Parliament banned virginity testing for girls under sixteen in the Children's Act, 2005.

India's Kanjarbhat Community has conducted and continues to perform virginity tests on brides for hundreds of years. Newlywed couples are expected to consummate their marriage on a white cloth; if the bride bleeds, she passes the virginity test. If she doesn't, it is assumed that she has had premarital sex, and the marriage is annulled. The Kanjarbhat caste council (all men) oversees the test.

Premarital sex is considered a moral crime only for women. In Afghanistan, women are jailed for failing a virginity test. Hundreds of women are in jail after having failed their virginity tests.

NPR reported in 2018 that virginity testing was a global issue. *Virginity tests have been documented in at least twenty countries worldwide, including Egypt, Indonesia, and South Africa. And according to the UN, increased globalization in the past century has resulted in requests for and cases of virginity testing in countries that had no previous history of the practice, for example, Belgium, the Netherlands and the UK.*

Government-run health clinics in the Philippines perform virginity tests, among other reasons, for financial reasons. Women willing to auction off their hymen at bars and strip clubs frequented by Americans, who pay more for sex with virgins, can acquire a V card or certificate of virginity at these clinics.

In the United States, according to a 2015 US Department of Justice report, between twenty-three and twenty-seven women are murdered in honor killings each year. In other words, more than two women are killed every month by family members who consider her sexual activity immoral or unacceptable. The numbers could very well be higher. Honor violence against women, a concept so tightly held within families, so private, so cultural, so tribal, so impossible to quantify.

I wonder what would have happened had my hymen been broken the day mom took me to have the virginity test. There would have been tears and rage and guilt. She would have pelted me in the kitchen with questions about the perpetrators, the men who damaged me, los hombres que me perjudicaron. She would have nailed me vertical and trembling against the kitchen wall and I would have crumbled. I would have told her there was no kidnapping and no men had taken me anywhere. I was riding my bike and lost track of time because I was in love with Diego. And no one, absolutely no one, would have convinced her that sometimes hymens break, that sometimes girls are born without a hymen, or with a perforated one. That I couldn't account for the state of mine, hadn't even given it any consideration until that day, and come to think of it, didn't realize I had one. It shaves something off a girl to be that vulnerable, her body subject to nonconsensual inspection. It shaves something off a girl to realize that her body is a vessel for somebody else's ordinary fears—about getting old, being left by her daughters, ceasing to exist. It shaves something off a girl to understand that there are unsurmountable limits to what she can do, but no limits at all to what can be done to her.

In honor cultures, women suspected of immoral behavior get killed by a relative, usually a male, as a way to save the family's face. Women are expected to conform to their elders' wishes, who are presumed to act for the greater good of the family. But Colombia is not nor has ever been an honor culture. Not officially anyway. What would mom have done? Surgical hymen repair was not an option in the seventies, and she would not have forced me into marriage. I have an inkling, though. I think she would have gone silent, denied me eye contact, and sent me into exile right there inside our little apartment. Her silences only broken by dramatic sighs within earshot just to remind me of the unbearable pain I inflicted upon her by not being a virgin. And I would have cried my eyes out, gone on my knees and sworn in the name of Jesus, Mary, Joseph, Saint Gregory, the alms of purgatory, and the eleven thousand virgins that no one had ever touched me. And she would have looked away and said nothing.

That night, thirty-two years ago, mom and I sat in front of our black and white TV. We didn't talk about the incident in the doctor's office. She offered no apology, no explanation. She didn't cook my favorite food, bake cookies, or make me a milkshake; she was not that type of mom. She was the unapologetic type. The kind that pushes forth even if wreaking pain and havoc on her path. She was a hardy woman, a manly woman, a no-nonsense kind of mother, a get-up-dust-yourself-off and move on, por el amor de Dios. Neither of us spoke and her silence told me she expected me to be a hardy woman like her. To stop crying and move on, for God's sake. I wanted to tell her that right up to this morning, I had felt as though I was moving toward something momentous, womanhood, but she had reversed the process, she had undone me, stunted my growth, and placed a hurdle on the road I didn't know how to circumvent.

Mom, as fate would have it, the memory of that day, of that minute, evaporated with time. It didn't haunt me. It didn't revisit me in the form of night terrors. It didn't create a chasm between me and the boys of my youth or, later, the men I loved. I dredged agency from the Marianas trench of the mighty fortitude I inherited from you, learned to own my body and shared it with whom and when I pleased. I welcomed my lovers' bodies with eagerness, with lust, with hungry curiosity. I learned to take and to give in equal measures, and no one, no one, ever placed his fingers near my oval without my invitation. Mom, the memory of that minute of silence didn't rob me of my ability to enjoy my sexuality. It didn't make me promiscuous or frigid. I don't choke thinking, talking, or writing about it. The thirty-two years that followed that minute have been filled with blessings and hiccups, but mostly blessings. I have no triggers, no signs of trauma. Ultimately, I did what you would have liked me to do: I pulled myself up by my bootstraps, shut my mouth, and moved on, por el amor de Dios.

2

Sheila Chandra's Silence

It would be glib to say that Sheila Chandra lost her voice. To lose something implies the possibility of finding it again, an exercise in determination to locate the misplaced thing as if the infinitive form of the verb held a redemptive power. Sheila Chandra did not lose her voice. A fire ravaged her throat, taking her voice with it as collateral damage.

The first time I heard Sheila Chandra, I was dating the wrong man for the wrong reasons. I watched the official video for "Ever So Lonely" on this man's TV. The studio had been set to resemble the Indian desert. It had sad-looking dunes made of fabric, an Arab cameleer, two live camels, four musicians, and sixteen-year-old singer Sheila Chandra. Draped in a purple sari, an elongated red bhindi stamped between her impossibly beautiful eyes, she swayed her hips in a fusion of Indian Punjabi and Western pop styles. The wrong man I sat next to indicated that if I were to remain his girlfriend, I would add Sheila Chandra to my playlist immediately. I was in my twenties, lost, and nearly convinced that to be seen by him was the pinnacle of my existence. Two years later, I left him, his violent hands, his peacock gait, and his collection of New Age music, including Sheila Chandra's debut album *Monsoon*, containing "Ever So Lonely."

The next time I saw her on TV, she performed at World in the Park, an eclectic music concert held in 1992, when I was living in Alaska. It was winter, Anchorage was the whitest patch on the earth, I was sitting on a thick rug, logs slowly burned in the fireplace, and I had my six-year-old daughter's head resting in my lap—one of those close-to-perfect life moments. The blue light from the TV gave the room an electrifying ghost-like ambiance impossible to ignore. Then Sheila appeared on stage, the second phantasm of the night. She wore a white kurta ensemble, a concentrical white and red bindhi on her forehead, making her thick eyeliner not excess but a necessity that gave her eyes an omniscient air. Sheila sat on a wooden patla, her knees on the floor, her hair fell on her right side all the way to her knees, the most splendid Rapunzel ever conceived, and there, half-seated half-knelt, she sang "Ever So Lonely" a capella. This was not the same adolescent shimmying to the Punjabi-Western pop fusion I had watched with the wrong guy. She was a woman, no longer a girl; her voice was pure, controlled, went all the way up there, mingled with meteors and nascent stars, then came low and sank into the horizon, giving me compassionate silent pauses to catch my breath. This was a mystical song, something for temples, shrines, pilgrimages, and living funerals. My skin was all goosebumps and quick tremors. Then she sang in tongues. *In tongues.* Unlike the Pentecostals, whose trances I always perceived as more histrionic than spirit, Sheila's chant hit a chord within me. She tugged at my heartstrings, possessed me, punched me in the gut, and left me immobile, all tears and emotion. She sang, not to me but through me, and awakened something divine I didn't know I held inside. I lay my hands on my little girl's head, feeling healed and like a healer.

In the fairy tale *The Maiden in the Tower*, Rapunzel sings from the cell where either a sorceress or her father—depending on which version one reads—holds her captive. A prince wandering in the forest hears her singing and is instantly bewitched. He uses the same call as her captor to access her cell.
Rapunzel!
Rapunzel!

Let down your hair
That I may climb thy golden stair!

He climbs her seventy-foot braid, they fall in love, and from then on, he visits her every night. They conceive twins, and the captor discovers the hostage is pregnant, chops off her braid, and casts her into the dark forest to die. On the same evening, the prince returns to visit Rapunzel at the tower, her captor flings the braid out of the window to trick the prince into climbing to the top, where the truth of Rapunzel's fate is revealed. The prince, overcome with grief, throws himself from the tower and survives the drop, but falls into a bush of thorns which pokes his eyes out. Blind and heartbroken, weeping and wailing over the loss of his lover, he wanders in the forest for a few years until, one day, he hears a familiar voice. It is Rapunzel who, with her twins, has miraculously survived ignominy. They run into each other's arms, two of her tears fall into his eyes, and the prince's sight is restored. Needless to say, they live happily ever after. And all this happened because Rapunzel had magic in her throat.

In *Tangled*, Disney's version of Rapunzel's story, her twenty-yard-long braid glows bright gold when she sings a special song, "Healing Incantation." This song has the power to heal the sick and wounded, make the blind see again, bring the dead back to life. Has Sheila listened to it? I want to think she has. That she played it and sang along, not wounded by the betrayal of her body, but brandishing her silence like a dagger, challenging the Fates' cruel design to turn back time, to bring back her voice, or else.

In 1992, Sheila Chandra had a near-fatal car accident in which she nearly lost her sight. To save her eyes, she was intubated, a clumsy procedure that resulted in a twisted larynx and a scarred vocal cord. Then started her silent march. She could still sing; in fact, she sang for another sixteen years, but life between concerts began to quieten her voice. Her singing practice time was reduced to one hour a day for a week before a show. This translated into her inability to talk to anyone for a week. In an interview, she explained, "That was all the vocal time I had without pain: two or three hours of talking or one hour of practice. I would go whole summers when I wouldn't talk to anyone, which was very bad for my mental and emotional health. It was killing me."

After years of singing with scarred vocal cords, the constant strain tripped her nervous system into chronic pain mode. She was diagnosed with burning mouth syndrome, an incurable neurological condition characterized by pain in the mouth that feels like burning, scalding, or tingling. If she talks or sings, she suffers. The fire behind her lips is rekindled with each utterance. Her voice box atrophies if she doesn't speak and spares herself the scorching agony. An impossible conundrum for a woman whose livelihood and identity are in her mouth.

According to the Mayo Clinic website, symptoms of burning mouth syndrome may include:

* A burning or scalding sensation that most commonly affects your tongue, but may also affect your lips, gums, palate, throat, or whole mouth.
* A sensation of dry mouth with increased thirst.
  The discomfort from burning mouth syndrome typically has several different patterns. It may:
* Occur every day, with little discomfort when you wake, but become worse as the day progresses
* Come and go
* Whatever pattern of mouth discomfort you have, burning mouth syndrome may last for months to years. Some sensations may be temporarily relieved during eating or drinking. In rare cases, symptoms may suddenly go away on their own or become less frequent.

♦ Burning mouth syndrome usually doesn't cause any noticeable physical changes to your tongue or mouth.

Dear Mayo Clinic,

Sheila Chandra's symptoms did not go away or become less frequent. She tried to soothe her fire with turmeric milk and honey-soaked mangos, with iced infusions and Darjeeling teas. She tried acupuncture, hot therapy, then cold therapy, to no avail. The fire did not tarnish her numinous beauty, nor did it physically change her tongue or her mouth. They dried up, slowly, relentlessly, trapping inside their walls an ember burning in perpetuity.

I tell my friend about the singer's condition, which has rendered her mute. Although it is a shame, she believes things happen for a reason. When I ask her what the reason for Sheila's torturous silence might be, my friend shrugs her shoulders. According to her, God acts in mysterious ways. We go back and forth in a Q&A where I ask all the questions, and she gives me cliched answers that satisfy neither of us. After my friend leaves, I go upstairs to my office to listen to Sheila Chandra's CDs. I play "La Sagesse" and "Waiting," again and again, the motor of the CD player whirrs in the background. I think about my friend and God, but mostly God. I imagine him as a doppelgänger of Santa Claus, minus the rosy cheeks. He is white and tall, carries extra pounds around his belly, has a long beard, and a wicked sense of humor. He is a childlike God. On good days when He is on his best behavior, He grants gifts at will. He allows Beethoven to create beautiful music, making him a virtuoso known and loved by everyone. Then when the man is twenty-six, He starts taking away his hearing, slowly—human tragedy is funnier in slow-mo—waits until the composer is in his forties to turn him completely deaf and implants in his brain and heart the music for Moonlight Sonata, an opera, and six symphonies, all of which Beethoven composes with his ear to the ground, desperately trying to hear-feel the vibrations of his own genius. God tries not to chuckle when at the premiere of Beethoven's Ninth Symphony, the orchestra replaces the maestro with another conductor, Michael Umlauf, who stands next to the composer but tells the performers to follow him and ignore Beethoven's directions. God's shoulders are shaking. He is having a good belly laugh. Oh wait, God makes the premier outstanding, the symphony receives rapturous applause, but He makes sure that Beethoven can't hear any of it. God instills pity in a contralto's heart; she approaches the maestro and turns him around to face the audience, to see the ovation. God is laughing so hard; He nearly falls off His divine chair.

Giving a gift only to take it away is not mysterious; it's heartless.

Grant Monet his gift, then give him cataracts. God is slapping His heavenly thigh, stomping His right foot. Give Van Gogh his gift, then give him madness, overdoses of digitalis and absinthe, let his xanthopsia color his paintings yellow, make him chop off his own left ear, then watch him kill himself at thirty-seven.

I'm not mad at God; that would mean that I believe in His existence. I'm angry at my friend for shrugging her shoulders when the world should hold a daily minute of silence with half-staff flags. Don't get me wrong, I'm not appropriating Sheila's pain. I candidly and deliberately rely on metaphor, allusion, hyperbole, tone, and other literary devices to place my imagination in the vicinity of her quotidian pain. I'm not being melodramatic either. I'm mourning the demise of her voice, although Sheila is not dead. I am a terrible fan, a mean fan, a needy, infantile fan who just wants to hear her voice again. She has transplanted her vocal sound to her fingers, and now she types life coaching lessons and books about creating order in chaotic times. But I'm not interested in that.

Sometimes, I close my eyes, and I'm twelve again. I am part Sheila Chandra and part Rapunzel; I have the former's voice and the latter's healing power. I'm on stage, dressed in a white kurta, half kneeling/half sitting on a wooden patla, my Rapunzel's hair cascading down the right side of my body, a bicolor bhindi planted on my forehead, and the heavy eyeliner, a necessity, not an excess, gives my eyes an omniscient air. I am also in the audience, waiting to be lifted, upgraded from merely human to a healer, and be healed in the process. I am both spectator and artist, a wretched woman and a goddess. She sings "La Sagesse (Women I'm Calling You)" and all the women of the World hear her call. They come all the way from Los Andes and the Himalayas, the Caribbean and the North Sea, the Arabian desert, and the Nordic fjords. She repeats the lines about our wisdom and our spirits, and the women in the audience roar. *Our wisdom cannot be lost, and our spirits cannot be broken.* And because I'm twelve and little girls do this sort of thing, I break out in my own Rapunzel voice, lay my healing hands on Sheila's throat, and sing with all the devotion I can muster: Bring back what once was hers.

3

Naked

It was 1983; the song "Every Breath You Take" peaked at number one on the Billboard Hot Ten. It was the year of more answers than questions for us. It was the year Victor asked me to show him my body. He wanted to reassert his sexuality. I said "yes" so that I could exercise mine. We discussed the meaning of Reassert and Exercise and decided these words expressed precisely what we wanted to do.

We were seventeen, had met six months earlier on our first day of college, and I had wanted to be his girlfriend ever since. Maybe because we were the youngest in the petroleum engineering program, were equally geeky, shared a penchant for big words, and despised macho culture with paralleled intensity, we gravitated toward each other.

He was perfect for me, precisely the way I liked guys. Tall, on the skinny side, with dirty blond hair, soft hands, an upturned nose that made me dream of ski slopes, and a smile that could fix all the world's problems. Victor had a few flaws that I was quick to forgive. For example, he had an unsteady walk that made him look like he was about to trip and fall on his face, could be extraordinarily aloof, and sadly, he couldn't dance, a shortcoming I was willing to overlook. But the eyes. God, I adored his eyes, the color of freshly minted pennies with little black rays shooting out of his irises like those of a golden eagle. His eyelashes were long, thick, curled up like choppy waters, and moved up and down with a sweet precision that made my knees buckle a little, not with lust, but with humanity. Often when he talked, I followed the rhythm of the lashes in favor of blabbering the not-quite-romantic-definitely-not-all-out-sexual-but-amazingly-strong feelings I had for him.

A few minor differences didn't matter much. I smoked a lot on campus (I wasn't allowed to smoke at home), flirted with anything with a pulse, cheated on my tests, and had a potty mouth. Musically, I loved hard guitar riffs, Alice Cooper, Kiss, Metallica; the noisier, the better. Victor didn't smoke, drink, cheat, or use foul language. Musically, he favored melody and paid attention to the lyrics of the songs. He was what people called a straight kid. A square I was determined to snug into my circle.

He arrived early with a bottle of wine and a box of chocolates. Straight away, he scored a ten out of ten on the chivalry scale. We put our cheeks together and kissed the air as we hugged. It was an awkward hug, but it felt like the first embrace recorded in human history. I opened the windows, and we both sat on a mattress on the floor. A light breeze made its way under my skirt, flapping it at the hem. I leaned back, locked my hands under my head, and let the breeze wash over me, from my naked toes all the way to the tangled curls of my hair. Victor was too nervous to notice. He moved his head right and left, scanning my out-of-town boyfriend's apartment.

First poem of the night: *Gaze upon me, my friend, pay attention to my body, for on it, in it, up and down, you'll find wondrous phenomena of the celestial kind.*

~

That night, away from the madness of a Medellín being ravaged by drug cartels, on the mattress I had shared with my boyfriend a few times before, I did not consider what I was about to do cheating. *It's not cheating if what you do, you do with a pure heart,* I reasoned, as Victor poured himself a glass of wine that we both knew would go untouched. I unwrapped a chocolate candy. Wrapped it right back.

After a long, awkward silence, he sat in lotus in front of me and looked me in the eye.

"I want to see you naked," he said. The words didn't just come out of his mouth; they rained down without preamble, like mean hail. No kissing, no foreplay. Just the business.

"You know I have a boyfriend," I said, to preserve Jimmy's dignity.

"What? I want to look at a naked woman."

My heart heard, "I want to see *you* naked," while my brain registered, "I want to see *any woman* naked." I let heart and brain wrestle for a few seconds, but that was when he pushed away a strand of hair that had fallen on my face; his finger left a trail of the cold night across my cheek, and I knew right there and then that I'd be naked for him by the end of the next inhalation.

∽

I was running different scenarios through my head when Victor asked me if I believed in love, as if love was a mythical figure, like the *chupacabras* or the Boogieman. I told him, Yes, and he said, Good, and one way or another, he ended up talking about how shiny my boyfriend Jimmy's hair was. *Hurry up*, I thought, *let's do this*, but I was too afraid to push him to the brim and scare him away. Instead, I played it cool and looked out the window at the sky. Planets, satellites, airplanes, everything up there looked like stars.

We both reached for the chocolates at some point, not because we wanted to eat them, but they were a necessary distraction, a delay of the impending. I held my breath when our fingers crossed paths. Victor sprang his hand away from mine, and some impulse toward self-preservation prompted me to retrieve my hand too. This step-less dance was beginning to wear me out.

~

I wore a peasant blouse with an elastic band at the neck. Discretely, I pulled the elastic down under my arms. Victor leaned over and breathed on my right shoulder when he discovered that my shoulders were naked. Could he smell last night's dreams still clinging to my skin?

He said that my right shoulder looked like a corner of Pegasus, but then he changed his mind when he found the space between my clavicles, which he thought was as wide as the distance between Alpheratz and Markab, Pegasus's bright stars. I had no idea what he was talking about, but nodded dutifully, then made the mistake of looking at his honeyed eyes, and my mind got stranded along the way. Every time he blinked, his eyelashes did something to me, the world went silent, and all I could think of were lazy monarch butterflies fluttering their wings after a long nap.

"Isn't that interesting?" he asked, and since I was already staring at him, I moved my gaze to his lips, which I noticed quivered a little. *Ha. I gotcha.* I wondered if lying next to me in the dark excited him. Then again, at seventeen, a boy shivering with cold can easily be mistaken for a man shivering with passion.

"Sorry. What?"

"Am I boring you?"

"Not at all," I said.

He rested his chin on my shoulder and looked me over from this angle. I bent my knees, let the skirt become a pond around my hips, and wondered if I looked sexy or if the hump on my nose was a turnoff. I stayed there panting lightly, as still as possible, not giving the slightest indication that I expected him to behave in a certain way, afraid that the magic would end if I twitched or winked. I liked feeling his weight on my shoulder.

Second poem of the night: *Dive into me, my dear friend. Parts of me lie on each side of my horizon; play on one side, drown on the other. I'm a nascent galaxy; come, I'll reward you with gems of unfathomable worth.*

~

"What does it feel like?" he asked me, as if trying to break whatever spell I was under.

"What?" I asked back, but I knew exactly where he was going.

"Sex."

I took my time trying to articulate the awkwardness of my sexual encounters with Jimmy, looking for words to encapsulate that most of the time, we didn't know what we were doing or were clumsy and inexperienced. I didn't want to tell him that we had lost our virginities to each other just a few months back. I concocted the most eloquent answer, which allowed me to sound experienced but not too slutty.

"It's slippery," I said, rubbing my index and thumb fingers together. "And you feel hot. You know, like you're running a high fever."

"Slippery? Is that it?" he asked with a forward jerk of his head, golden eagle's eyes wide open, eyebrows up high. "And the fever thing? I thought sex was a big deal."

I shrugged my shoulders. Slippery and feverish were the best I could come up with.

"I think a lot about sex," Victor whispered into the night.

"Me too," I said and swallowed hard. "With anyone I know?" I held my breath.

"Yes."

My heart beat so hard, so quick, I thought I would faint.

"Who?"

"With Daniel," he added matter of fact as if it were a known fact like gravity.

"Daniel, Danny? The guy in the calculus class?" I asked, pretending to be surprised, although I had already noticed how Victor got all giggly around Danny. "The architecture major?"

"Yep, that one."

Something within me split. I became utterly aware of my ordinariness, my unworthiness, my ugliness, my utter lack of sex appeal. I tried to say something, but I didn't want my voice to crack. I looked at the ceiling for a few seconds, bit the inside of my cheek, and tried my best not to bawl my eyes out.

"Say something," Victor prodded.

I cleared my throat. "You know he has a girlfriend, right?"

He nodded.

"That's messed up," I mumbled.

"Do you think I'm gay?" he asked.

"No, of course not," I said and prayed that he wasn't. I got up, made as much noise as possible, tossed things around, coughed, yawned, and slammed the window shut. A chilled breeze made its way into the room. I acted more annoyed by this detail than I was. I wanted to run away from the spot and dive into Medellín. That crazy, violent, beautiful valley.

"I dream about Daniel's chest almost every night," Victor said, and his words were so tender, so heavy with longing and confusion that I couldn't tell whom I felt sorrier for: him or me.

"I caress his chest, kiss it, and I come in my dreams," he said. "Every. Single. Time."

"Maybe you're going through a gay phase," I said, my mouth dry and sad. "I once French-kissed a girl, and I don't even like girls," I lied.

He straightened up and got closer. "I need to know for sure tonight," he said, looking at me over his shoulder. "It's tonight or never."

I took these words as a challenge. I figured that if I carefully treaded these waters, his waters, I could squeeze one *straight* night out of him.

～

"And the third angel sounded, and there fell a great star from heaven, burning as it were a lamp, and it fell upon the third part of the rivers, and the fountains of waters; and the name of the star is called Wormwood: and the third part of the waters became wormwood; and many men died of the waters, because they were made bitter." (Revelation 8:10)

～

It was almost 9:00 p.m. when we took our clothes off. I slipped my blouse over my head, unwrapped my skirt, shook it off with my legs, and left my panties dangling at my toes. Victor undressed methodically, like a dutiful husband. He removed his Lacoste shirt, his perfectly ironed Levi's, one white sock, the other, his cotton underwear, folded it all neatly, and placed it atop his backpack.

My breasts sprung to life in the cold night, protruding like pebbles stranded on a river bend. I braced for Victor's ravenous fingers, which he tapped on his chest like he was listening to Cyndi Lauper in his head. And when he didn't move, I reached out and brought his hand over. He acquiesced and spent a little time on the nipples, touching them lightly like they were on fire, then traced the areoles' circumference with a single finger before moving quickly to my mouth.

He spread my lips open with his cold fingers and asked if I thought a person could transmit cavities with a kiss because if that were the case, he'd never kiss anyone.

"I've got cavities," I said. "Kiss me and find out."

"You have a knack for grossing me out," he said.

We didn't kiss. Instead, I allowed him to continue exploring my face, closed my eyes, and let his fingers glide along my lips, in and out of my mouth, north and south of the opening, east and west along the edges of the precipice. I half-opened my eyes and caught a glimpse of his backpack and the Lacoste green crocodile sticking out its red tongue.

~

We were naked, sitting so close we could hear our breathing, the outer edge of his right thigh rubbing against my left one, and he wanted to know if I thought Danny had feelings for him. I wanted him to change gears from studying to enjoying my body, wipe that confused look off his face, turn around with a raging hard-on and tell me something real, not one of his theories about the cosmos. I shrugged my shoulders.

His fingers found my belly button a few minutes after nine. I tried not to shudder. On the ensuing recce, Victor found a couple of mosquito bites, one mole, three freckles, and a scar. He ran his index finger from my belly button to the pubic area and giggled.

"What?" I asked, and embarrassed, I covered my belly with both hands.

"Your *linea nigra* looks like you made it with a Sharpie."

~

I wished he'd just toughen up a little and talk like the other guys—tits, ass, fuck—pounce on me and breathe in my ear, my neck, hard and quick like Jimmy did. But he didn't make a move. And neither did I. Instead, I started to let go of the pretty picture that I wanted our friendship to become and accepted the reality as it was. I could draw sweet graffiti on his walls and write my two lame love poems on them with the right colors and in perfect proportions, but all of it would invariably wash away, revealing the core underneath it all—the stucco of his soul.

I thought about Jimmy's twenty-four-year-old body. Thick, muscular, hairy. The steely beard he refused to trim out of sheer laziness, the coarse hairs on his chest. Everything about him so unmistakably masculine. I turned on my side and looked at Victor. Hairless Victor, skinny Victor, chicken-legged, lanky Victor. I yielded to an empty feeling close to vertigo. Almost as if his incipient goatee and peach skin fuzz he insisted on calling a mustache had diluted whatever passion I felt a couple of hours earlier. His flaccid penis sobered me up. If I was addicted to his eagle's eyes, I quit stone-cold. I could not go on wishing for the apple tree to give me an olive. I felt my longing leave my body and rise to the sky; I imagined it like a trail of a zooming meteor riding away deep into space.

~

Victor didn't go beyond Venus. He hovered over it. He placed his hand on the mound, felt the pubic hairs tickling his palm, and said, "In-ter-es-ting."

He seemed to take mental notes as he analyzed my body—and therefore, every woman's body. He appeared to commit everything to memory as he stared at me with something far from joy and dangerously close to intellectual curiosity. He would have passed with flying colors if anyone had given Victor a test on me.

"I wonder what we look like from the sky," he said.

I tried not to sound bitter. "Probably like two loaves of bread on a bakery shelf or two slabs of meat on a chopping board."

"Why?" he asked.

"Never mind," I said.

We lay in silence, and in that silence, the proverbial veil lifted, and my body, free from the need to seduce and conquer, felt, if not content, at least at ease. Not raging with pheromones and goosebumps and below-the-belly earthquakes, but at peace. In that silence, I felt his love for me, the only girl who would get naked to satiate his curiosity. In that silence, I loved him with acceptance, with kindness so deep I didn't know I could feel, with the sort of love you carry in a pair of well-worn shoes, the love you take in a picnic basket to the park. Simple like a promise ring.

"Thank you," Victor said.

"You're welcome," I whispered, reaching for my shoes. I realized that we needed to set boundaries to remain friends. I couldn't trespass anymore. I wouldn't. The white-tailed deer had touched the electric fence, and she will never ever want to experience a similar jolt. I got all philosophical. I figured that his sexual orientation and my devotion conformed to my adolescent notion of the benevolent nature of love. I let the isthmus open between us and finally accepted that his waters and mine would never meet again.

I was inexplicably okay with it.

~

The last poem of the night: *And so I set us free from me, my friend. Steer away, for my love for you is pure solar heat, which might vaporize your radiant orbit's dust into a spark of oblivion.*

~

But that's not everything that happened. It is a modified memory, a version I have told myself for decades to soften the blow of that forty-year-old night. I'm the revisionist of my past. As the protagonist of my story, it is my prerogative to pick and choose whose attitude to previously accepted situations needs revising. This is what I remember. This is my emotional truth, the version I refuse to make official out of respect for our friendship.

Victor didn't go beyond Venus. He hovered over it. He placed his hand on the mound, felt the pubic hairs tickling his palm, and said, "In-ter-es-ting."

He seemed to take mental notes as he analyzed my body—and therefore, every woman's body. He appeared to commit everything to memory as he stared at me with something far from joy and dangerously close to intellectual curiosity. He would have passed with flying colors if anyone had given Victor a test on me.

"I wonder what we look like from the sky," he said.

I tried not to sound bitter. "Probably like two loaves of bread on a bakery shelf or two slabs of meat on a chopping board."

"Why?" he asked.

"Never mind," I said.

I felt my heart flop and shrivel, a sheet of rice paper left out in the rain. No, it wasn't the heart; this death was at the base of my ribcage where the diaphragm sits. It left my body without foundations, my whole being a figment of my imagination. Yet he didn't notice. My heartache, disillusionment, and humiliation were not variables in his equation that night. They were zeros to the left as he awkwardly tried to find a magic answer to his sexual riddle.

Victor asked if we could keep going. Keep going. That's funny because that's precisely what he'd done since the moment he walked in, a bottle of cheap wine in one hand, a box of cheaper chocolates in the other. He had consistently, relentlessly, and un-waveringly kept going, going, going away from me.

We had done the little anatomy lesson so tentatively, so un-sure of ourselves that it was only natural to him (not me) that we would proceed with the rest of the examination. No, let me rephrase; he didn't want to inspect me visually. It felt like his plan was to carpe diem me, to give my private me a thorough auscultation and rummage at will until he found his answer. A recce sortie inside the forbidden perimeter. He craned his head my way and gave me a little boy's inquisitive look as if saying, *ma'am is it okay if I touch this?* And asked me without words what exactly goes on within the folds and the pleats down there, where only Jimmy had been. He wanted to part the waters and dip his eyes into my sea, a Spanish conquistador plunging into El Dorado.

If this is what it takes, so be it. If showing you my most private me brings you over to my side, so be it. I'll open myself up. I'll show you what you want to see; let it prove that I trust you, like you, and love you more than I love Jimmy. We locked gazes in silence. His cheeks got bright and rosy as he moved in my direc-tion without taking his eyes off the prize. Everything happened in normal time, of course, but in memory, time elongates here, Victor's hands move in a dramatic slow motion, and I record everything for posterity. How he looked embarrassed, revolted, and curious, all in the same proportion. I noticed his delicate fingers and the soft, blond hairs on his phalanges. I memorized the noise he made when he cleared his throat before saying something unintelligible that sounded like a stutter, so not very sexy. I took a mental picture of his constrained face, like he was holding his breath, an amateur hunter about to fire his gun for the first time. I observed how my body instinctively clenched shut at the sight of his fingers so close to their final destination.

My flesh in one corner of the ring, my heart in the other, and no referee in sight.

This was it. We gave the wheel of fortune a good spin and waited with bated breath for it to stop turning. Gay or not Gay were the only two options we knew in 1983. This is the part of the story when I say that I let Victor in where he wanted to get, that his body stiffened in all the right places, his hands got ravenous, we dove into each other's mouths, and between sloppy kisses, I let out a theatrical *phew you scared me* while he wiped the sweat off his eyebrow, relieved. The sight of my naked body had dissipated the cloud. Hooray. The splendor of my open pleats and folds was all the truth he needed to know. What could Victor do but yield to the sexual prowess of my seventeen-year-old body, climb over the wall, and come to the land of my dreams, where we were exactly what each needed?

～

But this is different from how the night ended too. Which's why I need to retake the original version right where I said he moved his hands toward the forbidden perimeter. Something instinctual triggered my body to clench and shut. I could not, as Victor requested, keep going. I could not become a weak cocktail, three parts Victor, one part me. I refused to dilute my true self for curiosity's sake. As far as I was concerned, the anatomy lesson was over. He got his truth; I got mine. I had a rigorous mother, a strict curfew I was unwilling to break, and a bus to catch a few blocks away. I conceded defeat. No strategy would make me win this rigged game. We lay in silence, and in that silence, the proverbial veil lifted, and my body, free from the need to seduce and conquer, felt, if not content, at least at ease. Not raging with pheromones and goosebumps and below-the-belly earthquakes but at peace. In that silence, I felt his love for me, the only girl who would get naked for him and ask for nothing in return. In that silence, I loved him with acceptance, with kindness so deep I didn't know I could feel, with the sort of love you carry in a pair of well-worn shoes, the love you take in a picnic basket to the park. Simple like a promise ring.

"Thank you," Victor said.

"You're welcome," I whispered, reaching for my shoes. I realized that we needed that night to set boundaries to remain friends. I couldn't trespass anymore. I wouldn't. The white-tailed deer had touched the electric fence, and she never wanted to experience a similar jolt. I got all philosophical. I figured that his sexual orientation and my devotion conformed to my adolescent notion of the benevolent nature of love. I let the isthmus open between us; I finally accepted that his waters and mine would never meet again, and I was inexplicably okay with it.

~

The last poem of the night: *And so I set us free from me, my friend. Steer away, for my love for you is pure solar heat, which might vaporize your radiant orbit's dust into a spark of oblivion.*

4

Teaching Mom Long Division

I'm fifteen and convinced we can change the world for the better with the sheer power of education. The law in Colombia dictates that every high schooler needs to be a part of the literacy campaign by teaching one illiterate Colombian to write and read. My Catholic school has a few good niches for us to choose students from. Mine is a construction worker who earns a living at a brick factory. His name is Salvador, he is in his thirties, and due to financial hardship, he stopped attending school after fifth grade. He has crusty green eyes, bushy dark eyebrows, ill-fitting dentures, and halitosis, none of which seems to bother me when we sit next to each other at a makeshift desk his factory provides for him after hours. He is short and unassuming in the way our campesinos from forgotten villages behave. He covers his mouth when he smiles and walks with tiny strides, his shoulders too close to his ears and a chin too close to his chest of matted black hair. He is more eager than bright, but I knew from the first day I sat with him that his eagerness to learn would be the core of our relationship, not his intelligence.

Mom follows Salvador's progress. The longer I work with him, the more interested she is. She asks questions when I come home after my sessions at the factory.

"Is he not too old to learn?"

"No, Mom. Nobody is too old to learn."

"Is the homework hard?"

"No, Mom, homework is meant to be a reward for doing alone what he learned to do with me."

"Is he very smart?"

"No, not really."

"Oh, so he won't be able to finish high school?"

The idea of helping Salvador to get his GED has crossed my mind. It is a long shot for someone who hasn't opened a textbook in more than twenty years, but an idea worth considering. He has dreams that require education, so he works very hard. The first months are trial and error. I'm too young and inexperienced to know that there are different learning strategies. Still, I improvise, try flashcards, games, riddles, and we go over the same material many times until something clicks and opens a door in Salvador's brain. His ambition overrides his lack of mental dexterity. He struggles to do the work, but he wants more. I expand my rudimentary curriculum, alternate between Spanish and math, then add geography. A year after working with Salvador, getting his GED is within reach. I tell this to mom while I grade his math homework.

"What is that?" she says, looking at his notebook over my shoulder.

"Long division."

"I heard about it. What is it for?"

"It's when you have to divide a number by another number bigger than ten."

"And he can do that?"

I nod.

"You said he wasn't very smart."

"He is ambitious, Mom. He won't set the world on fire, but I'll do my best to help him get as far as he can go."

"What if I want that too?"

"What do you mean?" I ask, slightly confused. "Do you want to study *study* or learn long division?"

Mom shrugs her shoulders, unsure of herself. "I don't know. Both, I think. Am I too old?"

I look at her. Her short, wavy gray hair, perpetual rosewood nail polish, black flats, and tea-length floral dresses. She is only fifty but has always looked old to me, like a photograph. Old.

"No, Mom. You are not too old to learn. You are not old at all."

Now, besides schoolwork and Salvador's lessons, I need to make time for mom. We compare our schedules and agree to work every morning after breakfast since I go to school in the afternoon.

Mom has gone shopping for supplies in a belated back-to-school fever. She is now hunched over the dining table tracing margins in her brand-new notebook with a shiny plastic ruler, the price sticker still on, in her left hand, a red ink pen in her right one, the cap clutched between her teeth.

"You don't need margins, Mom," I say, trying to calm her anxiety.

"That's what we did in the two years I went to elementary school," she says, sounding disappointed. "And that's what you six children did in school."

I have confused her enthusiasm for anxiety. She is not anxious; she is eager, like Salvador.

I look at her from the other side of our round dining table. I'm reading an excerpt from Jean-Paul Sartre's *Being and Nothingness*. My philosophy teacher's assignment was to decide whether Sartre was a nihilist like Nietzsche.

Mom looks at the right red lines she has traced on the empty pages of her notebook and decides she needs left margins too. "Freedom is what we do with what is done to us," wrote Sartre. I'm processing his words, trying to break down this philosophical boulder into pieces my sixteen-year-old brain can digest, when I catch mom staring at the parallel margins. She smiles proudly. I can tell she likes what she sees.

"What's the hard bit for?" Mom is holding a gray and white eraser in her hand.

"The gray end, the hard part, is to erase pens and colored pencils. The white part can erase all kinds of pencil writing."

She irons the first page of her notebook with both hands.

"I'm ready," mom says as she puts the eraser into her pencil case. A pencil case. Something within me cracks right open, and the molten rock of my rebellious teenager heart, once hardened by angst and all its fiery substance, turns to goo.

For the next hour, I need to tread carefully. This fifty-year-old woman sitting next to me has a second-grade education, has not set foot in a classroom in forty-two years, and has never read a book, a map, or a compass. This is my student: a functionally illiterate single mother of six with veinous hands, svelte legs with spider veins on the inside of her knees, a bad back, dark lips, dentures, glasses, generous breasts, a perfect nose.

The next hour is critical. I can't push her too hard; I don't want to scare her away. I can't repeat myself too often; I don't want her to feel inept. I can't praise her too much; I don't want to be condescending. But I want her to understand our new dynamics. I am her teacher. She can't pull rank. Yet she is my provider, my source of spiritual and physical nourishment. She is my compass, and I'm not ready yet to set sail or be adrift. I know this much. I need to be very careful.

I start the long division process with multiples of ten and no remainders. I want mom to fully grasp the concept, master the basics, then slowly add more difficulty.

Mom excels at this. She gets all the divisions right and is getting cocky.

"It's so easy."

"Is it? It took me many years to learn this."

"No, it didn't."

"Did."

Let's get the basic terms first.

The **dividend** is the number on the right side of the equation, under the line. It represents the amount being divided.

The **divisor** is the number on the left—it's the one doing the dividing.

The **quotient** is the number on the top. It represents the answer or the number of units in each place value once the equation has been completed.

The **remainder** is the number on the top right. It represents the units left over that can't be evenly divided into the quotient.

My student looks befuddled. Mathematics is about numbers, not words.

"Can we get to the meat of it?" she asks, running her fingers through her gray hair.

This role reversal, the daughter teaching mom for a change, excites me more than I thought. First, I introduce an equation that doesn't have any remainders so she gets used to the format and starts understanding the new vocabulary she's just learned. I smile, giddy with her eagerness.

"You have five hundred pesos to spend on food for ten days. How much can you spend per day?" I ask.

"Is that what you are trying to teach me? I already know that."

I look at her, unmoved, and wait for her answer.

"Fifty, mija, fifty. I'm not stupid," she says, visibly annoyed.

"I know, Mom," I say, fully aware of her fragility, "but we need to cover the basics first."

We go back and forth with a few more exercises.

"If you have one thousand pesos to buy your five girls Christmas presents, how much do you spend on each?"

Mom looks exasperated.

"Twenty," she says and yawns to punctuate her boredom.

"Think again, Mom."

I grab her right hand in mine and tap each of her brown fingers. "Twenty, forty, sixty, eighty, one hundred. What happened here? You have 1,000 pesos, not 100."

Mom grabs her pencil, and just when she is about to write the numbers down, she mumbles, "two hundred, two hundred." She is embarrassed for getting it wrong, and I'm embarrassed for embarrassing her. I want to empower my mom, not humiliate her.

"But if you get confused, remember your mnemonics, DMSCBR."

We try the technique with the names of fruits but get stuck with fruits beginning with the letter R. We tried flowers, professions, and colors. We settled for animals. Delfin, Mico, Sapo, Cocodrilo, Burro, Ratón.

Divide
Multiply
Subtract
Check your work
Bring down
Repeat or Remainder

Delfin, Mico, Sapo, Cocodrilo, Burro, Ratón. Mom closes her eyes and repeats the mnemonic over and over. While she works at memorizing it, I scribble in my notebook.

Do you remember when you took me to a virginity test and stood right there behind the gynecologist, peering into my most intimate me?

Mao-Tse-Tung wasn't my boyfriend. Neither was he interested in taking my virginity. The little red book I hid from you, and you tried your hardest to find, was not a compendium of secret love letters but his communist manifesto, which, truth be told, I never understood. Still, the mere act of owning, carrying, and hiding it from you made me feel smart.

San Gregorio is not a saint, Mom. I'm sorry to burst your bubble. He hasn't been canonized yet, and he didn't perform surgery on my eyes. On my night table, you left cotton balls, a shot of rubbing alcohol, and some pennies to pay for his divine intervention. I used the cotton balls for a school project, put the pennies in my piggy bank, and the alcohol simply evaporated. There was no miracle, Mom, just chemistry and teenage scorn.

Closure means finality, a letting go of what once was. My father abandoned me and you and my five siblings. Take off your wedding ring, for goodness' sake. Let him go. Your wedding ring, your Catholic marital vow, the longing in your eyes when you sit in your plastic chair in the kitchen looking out will not materialize him. He is not coming back. Do something. Find closure. Let go.

Black, white, and native (not Indians, Mom. Indians are from India). We are a mixture of the three lineages. So when I fill out school forms, and you instruct me to check the box that identifies me as white, you deny me my true provenance. You want me to annihilate the Black and the native in me so I can be what I'm not: white.

Regla, you call our menstrual cycle a ruler. I used to think that a ruler was only this plastic thing I used in school to draw straight lines or measure distances. I'm older now. I know better. Ruler, as in a person exercising government or dominion over something, is a euphemism for menstruation. As if it was this cycling bleeding that defines a woman. You no longer menstruate. Have you stopped being a woman? Wait, you no longer have a ruler. Does this mean you are free?

I title my lousy acrostic "A Mnemonic of Past Grievances," tear the page off, and on the following page—still fresh with the imprint of my complaints, I start preparing mom's lesson. I want her to digest this at her own pace while I'm in school, and she is under no pressure to perform.

"Okay, this is a step-by-step example of a long division with remainder. Ready?"

Mom makes the scout sign with her fingers. "Siempre lista."

$$32 \overline{)\ 487}$$

"Mom, remember to set up the division problem with the long division symbol or the long division bracket. Put 487, the dividend, on the inside of the bracket. The dividend is the number you're dividing. Put 32, the divisor, on the outside of the bracket. The divisor is the number you're dividing by."

I wish there was an easier way to teach her this. Something with less talking, more fun, less rigid. But I don't know any other method. I plod on.

Divide the first number of the dividend, 4, by the divisor, 32.

Four divided by 32 is 0, with a remainder of 4. You can ignore the remainder for now.

$$\begin{array}{r} 0 \\ 32 \overline{)\ \underline{4}87} \\ 0 \end{array}$$

Put the 0 on top of the division bracket.

$0 * 32 = 0$

This is the beginning of the quotient answer.

After almost two years of hard work with Salvador, he asks me to help him prepare for his GED test. He is the sprinter at the finish line. He can see it, and he is pushing me to push him harder. He works almost feverishly. He knows the capitals of every country in the world. He knows rivers and mountain ranges. He knows words like chlorophyll, plankton, and pollinate. He knows the states of matter and the solar system. He knows about regular and irregular verbs and can recite the twenty prepositions of the Spanish language. Sometimes he looks so overwhelmed that I doubt there is any room left in his brain to store more information. He is not good at processing new material but excels at memorizing everything I feed him. His knowledge is deeper and broader in scope than when we met, but not enough for a GED. I know this. Yet miraculously, he passes the test.

"Did he pass the test?" Mom wants to know.

"He sure did."

"So, basically, he went from illiterate construction worker to a bachiller."

"Amazing, right? Salvador is a charging bull, Mom. I just cleared the way for him to push forth."

Mom listens to every word I say as though she doesn't want to miss anything. Like if she blinks, she'd miss some vital information.

I don't tell her the literacy campaign is particularly lax when granting GED certificates. The powers that be have lowered the standards so that more people can graduate and make the campaign appear like a huge success.

"I want to finish high school too."

We are sipping café negro in the kitchen. Mom is sitting in her white plastic chair by the small window, and I'm leaning on the sink and looking at the same totumo tree she is staring at. I'm trying to reconcile these three degrees of high-schoolness. Salvador and mom, both functional illiterates who haven't been in a classroom in decades, and me, who, at sixteen, has spent ten consecutive years, without a single day of absence, learning. The three of us getting our high school diplomas at the same time. Unfathomable, fantastic, absurd. Why the hell not?

Mom reads well, writes with elegant curlicues that remind her of my dad's ornate writing, and has remarkable reading comprehension skills. She is a fast learner, but her memory is fickle.

Somedays, she forgets as fast as she learns. Maybe it has nothing to do with her memory and more with her lack of focus and being a single mother of six with a monkey mind forced to multitask. Just the other day, we found her wallet in the refrigerator. My sister and I stood there openmouthed, staring in disbelief at mom's blue leather wallet sprawled open between the margarine and the tub of lard. She does funny things like this all the time. I must remember her forgetfulness and constantly remind myself that mom is not Salvador. They are two different types of learners, and she is my blood. I must cut her some slack, more than I did Salvador. Mom and I have something very good going on—our relationship is on a long-standing honeymoon, and I don't want to do anything to jeopardize our finally-found, desperately-needed harmony. We sit at the table like two war veterans, carrying the wounds we inflicted on each other in the previous years but keeping them secret. Let bygones be bygones. My rebellions, her mistrust, my anger, her almost comical fear of watching her last little girl become a woman. All water under the bridge.

Next, multiply 0 by the divisor 32 and insert the result 0 below the first number of the dividend inside the bracket.

$$
\begin{array}{r}
0 \\
32\,\overline{)\,487} \\
-0 \\
\hline
4
\end{array}
$$

Draw a line under the 0 and subtract 0 from 4.

$4 - 0 = 4$

$$
\begin{array}{r}
0 \\
32 \overline{)\ 487} \\
-0 \\
\hline
48
\end{array}
$$

Bring down the next number of the dividend and insert it after the 4 so you have 48.

$$
\begin{array}{r}
01 \\
32 \overline{)\ 487} \\
-0 \\
\hline
48
\end{array}
$$

Divide 48 by the divisor, 32. The answer is 1. You can ignore the remainder for now.

$48 \div 32 = 1$

Note that you could skip all previous steps with zeros and jump straight to this step. You just need to realize how many digits in the dividend you must skip over to get your first non-zero value in the quotient answer. In this case, you could divide 32 into 48 straight away.

$$
\begin{array}{r}
01 \\
32 \overline{)\ 487} \\
-0 \\
\hline
48 \\
32 \\
\hline
\end{array}
$$

Put the 1 on top of the division bar, to the right of the 0. Next, multiply 1 by 32 and write the answer under 48.

1 * 32 = 32

When I was a little girl, my mom had kidney surgery. The surgeon botched the stitching and left mom with a long jagged scar across her right side. The diagnosis was a case of a drooping kidney. The surgeon lifted it. Or so the story goes. I think the kidney was stolen, as the poor women's organs used to be when under anesthesia. Mom had endometriosis. Many years ago, she had a hysterectomy. When my sisters told me that mom had had everything taken out, I thought she was empty inside. Her heart dangling like a pendulum into the void. Mom has a bad back. She gets up in the morning dragging her feet, her right hand on her lumbar, complaining bitterly about her dolor de cintura, "waist pain." Mom has astigmatism and presbyopia; she wears round bifocals. Lately, she has been having photophobic migraines. She first sees a little bright squiggle in the corner of her eye, some foreboding telltale that a migraine is about to hit her. Then she goes to her room, closes the curtains, and lies in bed. Nobody can disturb her, which is fine because I asked her if she needed anything one day, and I didn't like what I saw. Mom was catatonic, her eyes wide open and fixated on the ceiling, her gray hair Medusa-style on the pillow, mouth agape. Mom looked a little deranged, a little dead. The sight made my hair stand on end. I closed the door and waited for her to give signs of life on her own accord.

$$\begin{array}{r} 01 \\ 32\overline{)\,487} \\ -0 \\ \overline{48} \\ -32 \\ \overline{16} \end{array}$$

Draw a line and subtract 32 from 48.

$48 - 32 = 16$

$$
\begin{array}{r}
01 \\
32\ \overline{)\ 487} \\
-0 \\
\overline{48} \\
-32 \\
\overline{167}
\end{array}
$$

Bring down the next number from the dividend and insert it after the 16 so you have 167.

I use the same curriculum I designed for Salvador but at a slower pace. Mom is curious about geography, and since I told her that Salvador had learned the capitals of many countries, she wants to learn them too. I know it's too much. Teaching mom the capitals of countries she has never heard of doesn't seem fruitful. I suggest learning about Colombian geography first. Mom agrees. I wish she'd stop measuring herself up against Salvador.

"Okay, Mom, Colombia is divided into thirty-two states," I say, the Colombian map spread open on our dining table.

Mom leans over the table and locates a few states, Bogotá, the capital of Colombia, and the Atlantic, and the Pacific Oceans bordering our country to the west.

"This is Venezuela, right?" Mom asks, pointing at the bordering country to the east. "Your dad used to go there. He said it was like Miami, but he's never been to Miami, so who knows where he heard that." Mom sighs. Her longing for my dad is heavy, sharp, and so defined that it feels like the three of us are looking at the map.

I start at the northernmost tip of Colombia with La Guajira, the capital: Riohacha.

"Your dad used to say that Venezuela was/is very rich because of its oil. Apparently, you can make a lot of money there. That's why he went so many times."

It annoys me when mom talks about dad with such deep yearning. When she does, she doesn't seem to remember that he abandoned her and their six children and never looked back. And if he ever made money, we never saw a penny of it. Really. What's wrong with her?

I ignore her comment and slide my finger out of La Guajira and into the next state to the south, Magdalena; capital: Santa Marta.

"Mind you, men are such liars, especially your dad, and women are so stupid; we believe everything they say." And just like that, mom goes from unrequited love, theatrical sighs, and dreamy eyes to pure scorn. "Maybe instead of Venezuela, he was with his 'amiguitas' while I waited for him to come back from his 'travels' like the boba I am."

C'mon, Mom, focus. I look at the clock. I've got the Sine and Cosine Rule waiting for me. I also have homework to do. *If I don't get my hypotenuse, adjacent, and opposite sites right, I'll fail my trigonometry test, and then I won't be able to blame it on your lack of concentration.*

While mom rambles some more about dad, men, and deceit, I list the thirty-two states and their capitals alphabetically. Mom looks at me sideways and over the rim of her glasses, as if saying, Are you listening to me? Are you learning about men? I do question mom's knowledge of men. She has known only one, so she is an expert on dad and dad alone. He is one man among gazillions of men. He doesn't represent his gender. I hope. We try a few states and capitals: Amazonas, Antioquia, Arauca, Atlántico, but mom is getting tired. We don't make it to Bolívar.

$$
\begin{array}{r}
015 \\
32\,\overline{)\,487} \\
-0 \\
\overline{48} \\
-32 \\
\overline{167}
\end{array}
$$

Divide 167 by the 32. See a pattern emerging?

167 ÷ 32 is 5 with a remainder of 7.

$$
\begin{array}{r}
015 \\
32\,\overline{)\,487} \\
-0 \\
\overline{48} \\
-32 \\
\overline{167} \\
\overline{160}
\end{array}
$$

Put the 5 on top of the division bar, to the right of the 1.
Multiply 5 by 32 and write the answer under 167. 5 * 32 = 160.

It's Saturday morning. No school for mom. Instead, she takes me on a "secret" foray. Mom is very clear about the number of knocks on the door. One, wait, another one, wait, now three consecutive ones. We hear some rustling on the other side of the door. Mom looks over her shoulder. I also look over my shoulder, right and left, although I don't know what I'm looking for or what will happen to us if we get caught. Her paranoia is contagious. Mom instructs me to repeat the knock. The letterbox opens, and I instinctively crouch to peer in, but mom pulls me back, shaking her head no. A man whispers from the other side of the letterbox, "Cuantos?" Mom says, "Dos," as she squeezes my hand nervously. A few seconds later, the letterbox opens and spits two thin rectangular boxes wrapped in newspaper. Mom throws a few crumpled pesos into the opening, and we speed walk to the bus stop with our contraband of Marlboros.

Mom resells the cigarettes at our apartment, where she runs an unauthorized shop. She also sells candy, chips, chocolate bars, sodas, and alcohol. She doesn't condone smoking or drinking, but selling either doesn't conflict with her principles one tiny bit. It is ancillary income. She claims that my sisters' financial contributions are not enough. I suspect they are, but mom runs this shop because she wants a taste of financial independence. Mom says that conducting business from her apartment is not illegal, doesn't need a permit or license, and to avoid confusion, she doesn't call it a shop; she calls it a Chuzo. El chuzo comprises a few shelves right behind the dining table, which means we have to sacrifice one chair, and now we have only three places instead of the intended four. Like any shop, this one requires bookkeeping. Since mom is profoundly mistrustful of financial institutions, she keeps her cash in plastic bags hidden in her underwear drawer and her accounting in a small notebook. She names her main account after herself, Carmen, and uses its meager funds for the important stuff. She calls her secondary account Carmelita and uses its even more meager funds for little indulgences. Carmen often lends Carmelita money or vice versa; one doesn't pay the other, and the moneys go from one plastic bag to another. Mom creates a third account to arbitrate. She calls this third account Carmaughters, a portmanteau of Carmen and daughters, Carijas. When mom is not looking for her wallet or her bifocals, she constantly asks me, "Did Carmen pay Carmelita? Did El Chuzo borrow from Carijas? Are Carmen and Carmelita in good standing?" ad infinitum.

$$
\begin{array}{r}
015 \\
32 \overline{)\ 487} \\
-0 \\
\overline{48} \\
-32 \\
\overline{167} \\
-160 \\
\overline{7}
\end{array}
$$

Draw a line and subtract 160 from 167.

$167 - 160 = 7$

$$
\begin{array}{r}
015 \\
32 \overline{)\ 487} \\
-0 \\
\overline{48} \\
-32 \\
\overline{167} \\
-160 \\
\overline{7}
\end{array}
$$

Since 7 is less than 32 your long division is done. You have your answer: The quotient is 15 and the remainder is 7.

So, $487 \div 32 = 15$ with a remainder of 7.

You would continue repeating the division and multiplication steps for longer dividends until you bring down every digit from the dividend and solve the exercise.

We've been working for almost three months; mom's progress is negligible. She eagerly comes to the dining table, pencil case in hand, the ruler at the ready, eyes shining with expectation.

"What are we doing today?" she asks me daily, clapping loudly.

"You choose," I reply, thinking she'll be more receptive if she chooses what subject to work on. But no matter the subject, with mom, every day is like the first day; her hard disk reformats itself and refuses to store new information. A clean slate. Mom's short-term memory is impaired, and because some days she has no recollection of having already said or asked something, I repeat myself to exhaustion. Her emotional need for company and interaction overrides her need for information. I make a point of being as loving, compassionate, and tolerant as I can be at my age, yet on a couple of occasions, my frustration forced me to excuse myself, go to the bathroom to muffle a scream, wipe a tear or two, and splash water on my face. I want this for mom. I want her to get her high school diploma, even if I must bribe someone and buy it. Then what? I ask myself. What would she do after? Apply to college? An impossibility. We work some more on the long division exercise, but the chuzo is busy today, and we keep getting interrupted. One liter of Coca-Cola.

"Remember your mnemonic, Mom?"

"Yeah, yeah," she said, writing down the sale in her crumpled notebook. "Perro, gato, burro, something."

"Ha ha, very funny."

I write Delfin, Mico, Sapo . . . don't make it to Cocodrilo. A neighbor wants four loose cigarettes and a lollipop. He says he is trying to quit, and sweets soothe his cravings. Mom rolls her eyes as she takes the four Marlboros out of a pack, vocalizes the word "stingy," tacaño, so that I can see her, puts on her the-client-is-always-right smile, puts the change in a jar, comes back to the table, writes the sale down, and looks at me apologetically.

"Now, where were we?"

We lock gazes. I know mom is clueless. I know she doesn't remember what we were working on two minutes ago or what we did yesterday or the day before.

"Astrophysics, Mom, today we study astrophysics."

"Astro what? Astro delfin, Astro perro, Astro burro," she gives me a mischievous look. "How am I doing?"

Today she is my unruly student. She wants to sit at the back of the classroom and launch spitballs into her teacher's head. Today, she doesn't want long divisions or state capitals. Today she wants to sell knick-knacks and play. I have a shorthand quiz, chemistry homework, and college applications to fill out. We call it a day.

When I come back from school, mom is in a winsome mood. She wants me to go to my room immediately and remove my school uniform. I'm tired and dragging my feet. Mom is relentless. "Go, go to your room," she insists. I walk into my small room, turn the light on, and there, propped against my pillow is a Roberto Carlos LP with a handwritten note that reads: Para mi profesora favorita. Feliz dia del maestro. To my favorite teacher. Happy Teacher's Day. I love this Brazilian singer and can't wait to play the vinyl in our wall-to-wall Victrola. I hug her to thank her, but the embrace turns into something else. She starts to cry, and before I know it, I'm sobbing in her neck. This is the end of our student-teacher relationship. We both know this big dream of ours will not crystallize.

"You are so smart." She is cupping my face with both hands, and her tears make me want to switch lives with her. *I'll marry the wrong man and bear him six children; I'll be a single mom and carry the load on my shoulders year after year. I'll cook, clean, and teach five girls and a boy how to be decent human beings. I'll renounce the company of a man, kisses, hugs, love. I'll buy contraband and run an unlicensed chuzo from home. I'll do all of this with a bad back, bad eyes, bad knees, a drooping kidney, and terrible memory. Mom, you go to school, pass the finals, get your high school diploma next month, and fly away. Be.*

I want to encourage her, push her a bit more, maybe go to the literacy campaign headquarters and ask for different teaching methods. I want. I want. I want. This. For. Her.

"Thank you for trying, mija, but"—mom shakes her head—"yo soy muy bruta pa'esto." How can she say that? How can she say she is too stupid to learn?

I hold her in my arms and whisper in her ear, "Mami, mami, mami," because I don't know what else to say. I open my eyes and scan our small apartment. My sisters bought it for her, and it is the only thing mom has ever owned. Outside my doorless room is a short hallway that ends in the dining room. I can see the table from where we are. Her pencil case is ajar next to the math notebook. She must have worked on her long division exercise while I was in school. At what point did she decide to call it quits? How far did she make it? There is so much I don't know about mom, past, present, and future. I don't know that her memory loss is not a quirk but early-onset Alzheimer's. I don't know that my dad will return to her only to desert her for the second time and that when he runs out of money, friends, and lovers, and cancer ravages his bones, mom will welcome him back and care for him until his last breath. I don't know that in a few years, I'll marry the wrong man against her advice, will get pregnant, and will be back here in this still doorless room, will go on my knees and ask her to let me move back to the apartment with my baby. She will say, "No, I told you not to get married. You are a wife and a mother now. Go fight your own fights." All I know is that I should've taught mom to use a calculator rather than long division, that I pushed her too hard, and instead of lighting up the path for her, I blew out the few candles she had still going in her.

We loosen up the hug and wipe each other's tears.

"Mom?" I stop to debate whether to finish my sentence, but it's too late. The words spill out of my mouth. "Today is not Teacher's Day."

"Isn't it?" she says. "Well, it is in my house," and marches into the kitchen to serve dinner.

5

Belated Comebacks: Four Rants

Belated (*adjective*)
1: delayed beyond the usual time
2: existing or appearing past the normal or proper time

Comeback (*noun*)
1: a clever or effective retort; rejoinder; riposte

1. To the cop in Washington

It was a frigid February in Washington when I took a cab to Dulles International Airport after a week at the AWP conference, the USA's largest writers conference. The streets were frozen, not in a clean, charming, hot-cocoa on a white Christmas afternoon type of frozen, but in a grim, street grit, pissed-off drivers, mental exhaustion, I'm going to miss my flight type of dirty frozen. The sheer size of the conference, the flurry of readings, panels, presentations, the nights at the hotel in an unfriendly bed, and the brutal temperature had left me terribly homesick. And by home, I mean Qatar, a country a transatlantic flight away, for which I had paid a fortune. I was running late, and my driver, who didn't seem to understand a word of English, shrugged off my incessant requests to step on the gas pedal. Then it all went to shit. We got a flat tire, a job hazard I wrongly presumed all taxi drivers were prepared for. My cab driver's tools were not in working order. The car jack wasn't jacking anything up, and the lug wrench seemed to have been made in a Tonka factory. After spending an eternity on all fours trying in vain to loosen the tire, he came around and tapped on my window with an open hand. I think he meant five minutes. Or maybe he had five problems. Or he had fixed the tire and had come to give me a high-five. In response, I tapped my imaginary watch. I'm late. I did the universal sign for a plane; I'm going to miss my plane, begged him to call another taxi for me because I'm cheap and refuse to pay for a SIM card whenever I travel abroad. But his radio was among the things that didn't work in his cab. We stared at each other through the window. In my head, I was screaming, Do Something. He stared back as if saying, What do you want me to do? He opened the driver's side door, stuck his head in, and asked me to get out of the car. Reducing the weight of the cab by one hundred and twenty pounds, he seemed convinced, would solve the problem. I reached out for an autographed hardcover I used to protect my boarding pass and other documents I didn't want to leave in the car. I stepped out. The icy wind slapped me hard across the face. I hadn't been this cold since a bitter winter during a short stint in Turkmenistan.

I stood on the curb, bracing my precious book, sheltering it with gloved hands as if it were a newborn, while the driver repeatedly tried to remove the punctured tire. It started to snow. Wet flakes fell on my dark brown boho winter coat lined with faux fur. The hoodie did not cover the entirety of my head. My hairline was getting frizzy. I couldn't feel my toes. My high-top Converse sneakers and the legs of my jeans were getting soaked. I was dressed for a ride to the airport, not for the wintery outdoors. I readjusted my reading glasses on my nose and was contemplating my options when the police arrived. Thank God.

Dear cop,

You and your partner arrived in a time of need. Your patrol car, with its blue and white colors of reassurance, made me feel like the whole Washington Police Department got my back, like a fleet of brand-new taxis was on its way to rescue me, like it would be impossible for me to miss my long, expensive flight home. Thank you.

I couldn't see your faces through the tinted windows, but I was sure you looked like angels in uniform. Why you stayed inside the car while I froze my ass off on the curb is beyond me. I want to believe you were running the taxi's plate number, ensuring it wasn't a stolen vehicle used for a heinous crime. I've seen a lot of cop shows. I know you do this sort of thing. I don't know if you looked at me from the warm comfort of the patrol and saw something I was not. And while you did this for a few minutes, I kept staring at the window, trying to make out the outline of your bodies, beckoning you with begging eyes, trembling legs, and hardcover pressed against my chest for dear life. Then the waters parted. You stepped out of the car. I sighed with relief. Finally, thank you. But you reached for your gun when I stepped in your direction. Stop time. Let's think about this for a second. I thought your job was to aid me, a citizen in distress. I thought your job was to make me feel safe. Instead, you reached out for your gun. At some point, your fingertips must have felt the holster on their way to the weapon. Your warm fingers on a piece of state-issued leather, your thumb must have brushed your belt, a punch hole, the stitching of your belt loop. Such a tactile split second. Your sympathetic nervous system fully activated; fight or fly, minus the fly bit; only fight left. A startled Ridgeback, its hackles on high alert. Danger. Danger. This 5'5" woman on the curb could potentially be a Molotov cocktail, an Improvised Explosive Device, an arsenal of weapons of mass destruction. Under different circumstances, say, after reading my work at AWP, I would have taken these assumptions as the biggest compliments ever. But not that day, when you perceived a woman half your weight holding a book as a threat; not that day, when taking another step in your direction would have cost a bullet in my body.

Do not move, you said. Let me see your hands, miss. And the fact that you called me miss, not ma'am, infuriates me even more because it means that you saw me, really saw me; you had looked at me long enough to ascertain that I was not old enough to be addressed as ma'am. And no, it's not just semantics. I am a writer. I find whole galaxies of meaning in words. Here's the thing. You ordered me to keep my hands in plain view without realizing that before I turned to walk in your direction, I had put my right hand in the pocket of my coat while my left hand continued to hold my precious autographed book. What was I supposed to do? Taking my right hand out of the pocket would have been perceived as a threat, and you would have pulled your gun. *The victim appeared armed.* Did you expect me to put both arms in the air, go down on my knees, whispering with a trembling voice, Don't shoot. I'm a writer. Don't shoot, as if my love for words was the only credential worth hurling at your gun. The antidote to your fear?

I didn't move. It continued to snow. You walked in my direction, your hand on your holster, which made me wonder if your partner's hands were aiming his gun at me from behind the wheel. The flakes got drier and fatter. We exchanged pleasantries. You looked inside the taxi, studied the taxi driver, assessed the situation, commented about my wet Converse shoes, and asked civil questions about where I was going.

Qatar? Wow!! I have never met anyone from Qatar.

I'm not from Qatar. I am an American citizen.

I wanted to show you my blue passport, but I was afraid of moving my hands too quickly.

I also didn't want to reveal I was from Colombia, just in case you had beef with Latinos.

When I told you I was a writer, you asked me what kind of stuff I wrote. I wanted to tell you about women's rights and the plight of the undocumented in the USA. Still, I was afraid of looking subversive now that your parasympathetic nervous system had, mercifully, taken over and that you had, finally, smiled at something. You had good teeth, I remember. You softened; the rough edges of your face melted under the snowfall. You took my backpack and the books from the taxi and put everything into the patrol car. You introduced me to your partner, who drove me to your police station. You ordered me a cab. I made it to the airport on time. I didn't miss my flight. I made it home alive.

I often wonder what exactly it was that you, a big, badass guy with an armed partner, a badge, a uniform, and a gun, perceived as a threat. Were you afraid of the faux fur lining of my boho coat? A bad childhood memory, perhaps? Did my wet Converse sneakers look like they were hiding a bomb? Did you confuse the Chimamanda Ngozi Adichie book I held against my chest, like a shield, with an explosive vest? At what point did you size up my one hundred and twenty pounds against your, say, three hundred and decide I could kick your ass if you didn't draw your weapon? Was it my skin color? Did you have beef with Latinos? Or do you live in a constant state of fear and tremble at the sight of your own shadow?

According to police statistics, so far, there have been 103 homicides in Washington in 2020. I hope you haven't killed anyone or been killed. I pray all your encounters are ridiculous buzzkills like ours. I hope age and compassion have elongated the path between your fingertips and the holster. I hope all the exposed police brutality of this year has made you soft, a better human being, a man who protects good citizens and keeps the streets clean of the bad ones. I hope you remember the day you nearly shot a writer hugging a book and feel shame so acidic it burns your throat every time you swallow, shame so gooey you could bury your teeth into it. As I said, you had good teeth.

2. To the woman in Marshalls

During one of my trips back to the USA, I visited the Marshalls store near my home in Lakeland, Florida. I found a black tank top that read *Peaceful Warrior* in big white capital letters. It was the perfect piece of clothing to wear for my yoga classes. As an instructor, I regularly share inner peace messages and instill determination to awaken our inner warriors. I liked it so much that I decided to go back the following day to purchase a second one as a gift for one of my friends in Qatar. To avoid having to describe the tank top I was looking for in a store known for its chaotic clothes aisles of misplaced, usually crowded clothing racks, I decided to wear it.

Dear woman,

As I remember, you couldn't stop looking at me or my Peaceful Warrior top and, at some point, gave me a thumbs up over a list of color-coded discounts in the activewear aisle where you pretended to be interested in the same leggings I was. After following me with your piercing blue eyes for a long time, so long that I thought you were from loss control and had singled me out, as Latinx often are while perusing the stores, you walked in my direction with a smirk. No, you didn't walk; you marched with such determination that I stopped fingering the waistband of the leggings and returned your gaze with curious intensity. You stood in front of me, pointed at my Peaceful Warrior shirt, and proclaimed: that's an oxymoron. And I would have agreed with you had you taken a second to breathe before you said, But I don't expect you to know what oxymoron means, honey.

Whoa, whoa, stop right there, lady.

Our history is about forty-five seconds long. We entered into each other's fields of vision two blinks and a sneeze ago. Cram everything you know about me into the palms of your hands. Now, clap. That is the extent of what you know about me. What made you think I didn't know the meaning of the word oxymoron? And while on the subject, did you know that oxymoron is an oxymoron? Although the word has Greek roots, it didn't exist in classical Greek. Oxy-moron was constructed from parts that did exist way back then. The first half of the word oxy– means "sharp." The second half of the word oxymoron is –moron, and yes, it does mean "stupid" in Greek. Oxymoron means sharp and stupid at the same time.

That day in Marshalls, when you took me for a moron, you didn't want a rhetorical exchange. Yours was not an invitation to discuss semantics and etymology or contest your <u>allegedly certain</u> English language knowledge. It was a power trip. You wanted to declare your linguistic superiority in a public place, among leotards and yoga pants. You <u>acted so naturally</u> as if trespasses such as this were the only way you knew how to communicate with the world. In my book, words are sacred; therefore, semantical disagreements are holy wars. What did you see in me that made you think I didn't know the meaning of the word oxymoron? Was it my clothes? Did you look at me, study my black and white Peaceful Warrior top matching my <u>long shorts</u> matching the <u>rustic elegance</u> of a pair of wooden mules I bought in Prague, declare my style <u>shabby chic</u>, then proceed to insult me? Or did you look at me, guess my ethnicity, and your <u>only choice</u> was: stupid Latina?

Your assault, as effective assaults do, surprised me and left me <u>clearly confused.</u> I would have loved to be able to react, to say something <u>amazingly awful,</u> you know, some devastatingly witty comeback, and have a <u>bittersweet</u> moment of triumph with more honey than raw cocoa.

However, my mind went blank, <u>deafening silence</u> took over, and you and I stood <u>alone together</u> in the activewear aisle for a few painful seconds. Mortified and humiliated, I picked up a piece of clothing, I don't remember what, and joined the <u>small crowd</u> queuing up in the changing room.

Here's the thing. I've always been Slow to React to verbal abuse and microaggressions; it's an <u>open secret</u> among my family and friends. When under attack, I tend to <u>grow small</u>. I don't even get <u>passive-aggressive</u>. I instinctively start racking my brain, looking for some <u>random order</u> I can cling to, which can take me back to the <u>original copy</u> of myself. Alas, I always come up empty. This is why it has taken me four years to write you this letter. It is a hello and goodbye epistle, a <u>farewell reception</u> of sorts. I have included twenty oxymorons in this letter, one for each dollar you paid for that tacky <u>dress shirt</u> you must have deemed perfect. Truth be told, it was <u>pretty awful</u>.

3. To Karen, my ex-friend

Remember that day we were walking to Bonefish Grill and you caught your reflection in a shop window and complained bitterly about your weight and how hungry you were all the time because you had let yourself go after the divorce, were overeating and stopped working out and now guilt-ridden had gotten into the habit of counting calories whenever you had food in front of you and I told you that I thought you looked great, I honestly did, and you looked at me and said, Oh Girl You Don't Know What's Like to be Fat and I said, Well, I have always been thin, as if apologizing for the way nature made me and then you looked at me up and down and told me you'd kill to have my body and I was mortified for being complimented on something I had never worked hard for, but mostly I scrambled for words to soothe your self-inflicted wound and you repeated in case I hadn't heard you the first time that you'd kill to have my body and just when I was about to make a list of the body features you had which I had always wished for myself—big breasts, round butt, wide hips, you added, Except your Skin Color, but I didn't say anything because surely I had misheard you and anyway we were meeting more friends and the night was young, I was the newest addition to your group of uber cool middle-aged women, and I was in desperate need of friends. Besides, who would want to befriend a Latina with a chip on her shoulder?

Here's the thing. I don't know if you chose to be fat. I certainly didn't choose to be thin. All I know is that we are adult women, and among the few things we have control over are how much we move our bodies and what we put in our mouths. Genes, hormonal imbalances, and gland malfunctions aside, we are what we eat. Starving yourself and counting calories won't help the cause. Also, FYI, drinking five G&Ts before you go to bed, as you do, equals consuming almost a thousand calories. Just saying.

And the big one. You didn't get to choose to be white just as much as I didn't choose to be brown. That was something that our ancestors took care of many generations ago. I want to tell you a story: six million years before you or I were born, there was a great African mother ape named Pan Prior, out of whom chimpanzees and our line evolved. From that point, about fifteen different species of humans evolved until something happened about two hundred thousand years ago. *Homo erectus* evolved into *Homo sapiens,* and out of the few thousand women in this species, only one survived. Yes, Karen. Everyone alive today descends from this African woman. I know long stories bore you. Bear with me. Twelve thousand generations ago, you and I had one ancient mother. That makes us sisters. Kind of. This means that the ancestors you claim arrived in the USA aboard the Mayflower also had ancestors who had ancestors. You catch my drift.

The truth is that *Homo sapiens* came out of Africa and spread to Asia and Europe, and then some of them, about twelve thousand years ago yesterday, made it to America. I'm trying to tell you that your European ancestors came out of Africa and lived and died for many generations in the cold steppes of Germany, waiting for the Ice Age to end. But you will probably laugh if I tell you this because according to your flavor of Christianity, God created the earth and its white humans four thousand years ago. Evolution, to you, is a risible leftist fabrication. It doesn't matter. The archaeological record doesn't lie. You might lose weight (you don't need to) and become skinny, but you can't change your skin color or that of your ancestors. Remember, Karen; you were black before you became white.

Let this fact sink in slowly.

4. To the cholo who pulled me over on US27

Yes, I was speeding when he pulled me over. Guilty as charged. In my defense, I had been driving to Immokalee for almost four hours on US27. I was tired and itchy to get to the trailer park where I'd interview undocumented women for my book. If I didn't arrive on time, I'd be missing the one and a half hours the women had set apart to talk to me.

"Pull over," a man's voice said over the loudspeaker. *Oh, boy,* I thought. *This is going to hurt,* and I wondered how much the speeding fine was going to be. I put the gear into Park. He came out of his patrol and walked in my direction. The moment I saw his face and a second later, when I read his name tag, García, I breathed at ease. He was Mexican or of Mexican descent. A Latino like me. *Maybe this won't hurt as much. Phew!*

"Driver's license, please." I reached under the passenger's seat for my briefcase. "Slowly," he commanded. "Very slowly." I stopped moving, my hand still in the air, and I thought, *really, Hermano, you're going to be like this?*

"Whose car is this?" he asked, tapping the driver's door with something metallic.

I shook my head in disbelief. "Excuse me?" I asked, half insulted, half amused. It felt idiotic to keep staring at the briefcase, still under the passenger's seat, so I turned my face in his direction, locked gazes with him momentarily, and said, "*Mine*, of course."

"Okay, I'm going to ask you again," he said, visibly annoyed. "Whose car is this?"

I might have let out a little sneer.

"Do you think this is funny?" he asked as he reached for his radio.

"Is smiling considered a felony around here in . . . where are we again? Clewiston?"

And that was it. He called for backup, and in what seemed like seconds, my sunset Pontiac Firebird was surrounded by four police patrol cars.

Here's the thing, Cholo García. And I will call you cholo because whether you were born in this country or are a naturalized citizen, you can't hide your Mexican roots behind a badge. You tried your hardest to sound gringo, as if speaking nasal English was a desirable linguistic attribute around Lake Okeechobee. Still, your Mexican-English accent, your dental fricatives, and loans from Spanish phonology gave you away. Hear me out, Cholo, the chassis of your American-made patrol car—which is not yours anyway—would break into pieces under the weight of your Aztec ancestors.

This car is mine.

I am an anthropologist writing a book about the plight of undocumented Mexican workers toiling in the South Florida fields, and yes, I drive a sports car. And although you don't deserve an explanation, I'm going to give it to you anyway. I returned to this country after four years of living abroad, where I earned my PhD. That's all I had upon my return—well, that and a complicated immigration status that required a lawyer, which I could not afford because I was unemployed, not through lack of education but a lapsed re-entry permit.

Are you still with me? Fantastic.

I lived in a small community in rural central Florida, needed a car, but couldn't afford a rental. To tell you that I struggled is a gross understatement. One day, at my wits' end, I walked into a car dealer, and I said to the first car salesman to accost me: listen, I don't have a job, I don't have money, the banks won't lend me a penny because I have no credit history, but I desperately need a car. What can you do for me? And you know what happened, cholo? The waters parted for this Colombian woman. They had a Drive Away Today program and a low-interest car loan for recent graduates. The requirements? My dissertation, the original degree certificate, my social security, and a valid address. Guess which type of cars were available under this program. Pontiac Firebirds. Imagine that.

I became an American citizen; I got a job as an adjunct professor, worked hard, paid my car off, and bought a house by a lake. I mow my own lawn and keep the front yard pristine. I pay my mortgage on time, my taxes, my only credit card, and my utility bills. I buy knick-knacks from Goodwill, work out at Gold's Gym and the YMCA, love the Red, White & Boom Fourth of July firework displays, and cherish friends, family, and food every Thanksgiving.

Yes, this car is mine.

You seem surprised to see a woman driving a sports car, so suspicious of a Hispanic behind the wheel of a sunset Firebird that your immediate assumption was that the car belonged to someone else. Did you think I had stolen it? Maybe I or my Colombian cohorts—who could somehow be hidden in the tiny trunk of the car—used the Firebird to commit a crime? Did you think that I was somebody else's driver, a struggling Latina who delivers sports cars up and down the peninsula but couldn't, in her wildest dreams, aspire to own one? What gave you the right to doubt that I could drive something nice? You don't know me; you don't know where I come from; you have no idea how many fires I had to put out to place myself on US27 in front of you where you forced me to speed, then penalized me for it. What kind of shattered dreams forced you to make the tribal assumption that no one south of the border is entitled to the comforts of American life? Is that borrowed patrol car the crystallization of your American dream? Are your pals, the ones you radioed to help you defend yourself from a short and thin Latina, impressed by your display of power? Are they also frustrated, lonely Cholos like yourself, power-tripping in and around Godforsaken Clewiston, of all places?

Tell me where you live. I'll pick you up on your day off and take you to a good taqueria I know. In there, you won't have to use your put-on gringo accent or hide your insecurities behind a badge or a borrowed uniform. We will speak to each other in Spanish, our common language. You will say chinga, íjole manita, ándale, and I will say carajo, juemadre, berraco, and talk about our mothers with reverence and politicians with disdain. I will tell only the good about Medellín, and you'll pick and choose what to say to me about Mexico City. And we will laugh with our mouths open, rows of silvery fillings topping our molars, revealing that we come from countries that, unlike the USA, don't worship dental aesthetics. We will devour our food, yours with more chili than mine, have a couple of beers, and ask for the bill—my treat. Then, I'll give you a ride back home, drop you off at your doorstep, and drive away in my Firebird.

Yes, Officer García, this car is mine. *Mine*!

6

Getting Drunk with my Buddies

I need a drink. I have been dating an English man at a multinational oil company where I work as a petroleum engineer, and things have turned sour. He doesn't speak Spanish, I don't speak English, and other than the sex patois we use to communicate, there is nothing much keeping us together. That's not true. Sometimes when we hold hands, he buries his fingernails into the palm of my hand, leaving half-moon marks on my skin, a simple detail I have come to interpret as proof of his love. He wanted to possess me, and he did. I was, still am, his Pocahontas, a trite version of the civilized savage, who may or may not one day be taken out of Colombia and presented to English society as an example of the pretty third-world things an English geophysicist can get. But he has a fickle heart and no longer wants me. He has found another cute thing, and I feel like shit for not being able to retain him; for not being smart enough or pretty enough or sophisticated enough to make him want me in his life.

My Pocahontas braids are weighing me down.

So I go back to what I know: my buddies from college. I was the only woman in my classroom of twenty-plus studying to be petroleum engineers. After seven years of trials and tribulations, we became one big happy family where I was, still am, the little sister. In college, I was a young woman trying to make it in a man's world, and for that, I was ridiculed, discouraged, called a dyke, made the butt of all blow job jokes, constantly reminded of all the sucking and spreading I'd have to do to get a job in the industry. But as fate would have it, and against everyone's predictions, the haters had to eat their words. I'm the only one from my class with a full-time job at none other than British Petroleum, the most sought-after oil company in the country, where I get paid the whopping amount of five hundred dollars a month, more money than any of us ever dreamed of making. Unsurprisingly, I live paycheck to paycheck and even after almost a year of employment, I don't have enough savings to furnish the very well-located apartment close to the World Trade Center. That's okay. My buddies are unemployed, broke, and have zero home-decorating standards; they won't judge my empty walls or the mattress on the floor. They will be thrilled to see their little sister again and drink at her expense while at it.

I invite three of them. The ones in Bogotá looking for a job. I haven't seen them since graduation day, and it is a happy reunion. We kiss, hug, look at each other, and laugh like we just made it back from war miraculously unscathed.

We sit on the beige carpet that I have just vacuumed for my buddies and open the first bottle of aguardiente. I don't have shot glasses; we pass the aniseed alcohol around, taking swigs straight from the bottle like in college. We talk about the good old days and smoke my Marlboros. The realization that they are in my apartment, drinking my liquor and smoking my cigarettes, sinks in. I feel pretty badass. So this is adulthood. This is what independent women do; they shoot the shit with their male buddies and drink with abandon, recklessly, as if they have just been released from an indenture.

Remember when Professor X caught me cheating in the physics final? Ha ha.

Did you know that Y slept with Z during our junior year?

No way!

Oh my God, who remembers the guy who couldn't sleep for days the first time he was sent to the rig site and lost his shit through lack of sleep?

What? No, who was that?

Remember, he lost it. One night, he climbed to the rig site tower, had a panic attack at the crown, and had to be airlifted.

Oh yeah. His name was Pastor or something like that, right? Pobre güevón. Ha ha.

Hey, who was accused of blowing up the dean's Renault 12? He had just finished making the payments, right?

That was Pastor too.

No, it wasn't.

Yes, it was.

We burst out laughing and drink more.

To the dean, pass the bottle. To the dean, pass the bottle. Salud.

We finish the first packet of cigarettes.

Woman, don't you have any food in this house? One of them asks.

Be my guest, I say, pointing to the small kitchen.

There isn't much to eat in the refrigerator because I stop eating when I'm in pain. Depriving my body of nourishment makes me feel whole. Instead of eating, I drink more, smoke compulsively, like the protagonist of a cheesy telenovela. Maybe heartache is this self-consuming, this ravaging, this self-punitive because I am a woman. I don't know. My buddies are different. They don't seem to experience life with the same intensity. Things like unemployment, uncertainty, poor health, and low self-worth do not affect their appetite. They are always hungry. They raid the pantry and leave the fridge clean.

We open the second bottle, and I'm feeling mellow. One of my buddies asks if I have a good cassette.

Of course I do.

We play old salsa music, a few merengues, and the trovas Cubanas that filled our college hearts with all sorts of emotions. We drink some more. It's getting late. Too dangerous for tipsy young men to be in the streets waiting for a bus. We decide to have a sleepover like so many all-nighters we pulled while studying hard for a drilling test.

Juan takes off his shoes.

Man, have you heard of talcum powder? We pinch our noses and make gagging noises.

Pepe belches.

Carajo, Pepe. Did you eat mice for lunch? We throw Juan's shoes at him.

I envy the vast distance between my buddies' genitals and their hearts, their ability to fuck without falling in love. For seven years, I saw them cheat on their girlfriends, have flings, and pay for sex on field trips while I waited for them in the lobby of the town's whorehouse. They wouldn't understand my emotional turmoil. They don't have a job, bills, a sad unfurnished apartment, and haven't been dumped by a lover who speaks Yorkshire English—an accent unintelligible to me. The minutes become hours. My buddies appear more tender, more receptive, softer than ever, or perhaps I'm just drunker than I think, but before I know it, I spill my beans. I tell them why I'm so heartbroken.

They sneer.

About time someone breaks your heart, Antonio says. You broke all ours in college.

I did not.

You did too. You were the only girl. We all wanted a piece of your ass.

Nice to know, asshole. Thank you.

I slap Antonio hard on his arm.

We laugh, pass the bottle around, take long swigs. My vision and speech are happy blurry.

How about some dancing? One of them asks.

Why the hell not, right? I haven't danced to Latin music since I left college, and my feet get excited at the prospect of dancing with other Colombian men. But my boys choose *Sopa de*

Caracol, and because I'm the only girl and the song calls for some furious booty shaking while on tiptoes, I end up dancing alone. *Si tu quieres bailar sopa de caracol, hey!* I'm drunk and free of inhibitions. I think I can dance better than Vanessa Williams and Paula Abdul together. The boys go silent; I guess they are impressed. Juan looks at me funny. I stop and ask him.

What?

What, what?

Why are you looking at me like that?

Like that, how?

I don't know, funny.

They look at each other in that tribal way I learned in college to identify as their silent, secret code. Something that says *wouldn't you like to give her one? That's a fine piece of ass. Man, oh, man.*

I go to the bathroom to wipe the sweat off my face. Juan's gaze has unsettled something inside me. An internal alarm of sorts. My body is warning me, but I discredit the wisdom of my gut and splash cold water on my neck and face. Stop being so goddamned paranoid. I don't think of the consequences of not speaking out. These are my brothers, for fuck's sake. I'm confusing my buddies with the English asshole—two different breeds of men altogether. I walk past my intuition. I ignore my instinct, which is to say, I abandon my soul because if I don't, my buddies will abandon me, and I need them.

I go back to the living room.

Pepe has untucked his shirt.

Antonio's belt is on the carpet.

That's what you do at home. You get comfy. I'm pleased with myself because, somehow, I managed to make three men feel at home in this empty space.

The dancer is back, Pepe says excitedly. Que siga la fiesta!!! The other two cheer.

He stumbles on his feet, holds on to the wall for balance, and grabs my hand.

Let's dance, bizcocho, he says. Don't get any ideas about leading me, he adds. I'm the man; I lead. Pepe turns the volume down, and we dance to an old vallenato tune. I don't know what I hate most about vallenatos: the monotonous shrill of the acordeón, the singer's whiny voice, the incessant scratch of the guaracha, or the songs' excruciating length. With vallenato music, the couple clings to each other, barely moving their feet, breathing in each other's ears, rubbing bellies together. There is no room for creativity or fun. But Pepe loves vallenatos, and he rubs his belly against mine. I push him back, and he brings me closer; I let him, then get sweaty and bored, and I push him away again. The song is still on. Pepe brings me closer, only this time, instead of his belly, I feel a hard-on. I don't like where this is going. He makes a move to kiss me when the song finally ends. I decide not to make a scene and kill the mood; instead, I sigh with dramatic relief.

I thought it would never end.

Pepe gives me a wink. You are a fantastic dancer, mamacita.

As sad as it sounds, I like to hear that. A little recognition at this juncture of my life when nobody gives me the respect I think I deserve feels like a gift.

We open the third bottle.

My mind starts wavering. I feel like a mercury orb, light and bouncy but safe in my boys' presence. Who knew that the sight of their unkempt beards and scruffy clothes could feel this comforting? Juan places my head on his lap and presses the bottle against my half-open mouth.

One more drink and your troubles will be a thing of the past.

Nope. I move my head from side to side. No more aguardiente for me, I say. At least, I think I do. I don't want any more of that mierda, but also, I don't want to be the girl who can't hold her liquor, such a cliché. I drink anyway; for a girl sometimes it's easier to say yes than to say no. I light a cigarette and try to blow more smoke rings, but my lips are not responding. I miss the ashtray and extinguish my cigarette on the carpet. Oops. How funny. They all put their cigarettes out in the same hole, a drunken gesture of solidarity that makes us laugh and snort hard.

Someone pulls out a Polaroid. Who told them there would be an opportunity for photograph-taking? They snap pictures of everyone and everything. In one of them, Juan wiggles his tongue dangerously close to my mouth. In another one, Pepe is on top of me, not touching me, just pretending to do a push-up. I think. They take turns photographing themselves with me. The frames behind each of them remain unchanged, which means I am passed around. Like the bottle. A bit of aguardiente. A bit of me. I get a very uncomfortable feeling that I can't verbalize. My gut seems to know the words, but they won't leave my mouth. The world whirls around me. I'm the sun. Ma' boys are my very own planets, orbiting around me. I'm the center of their solar system. One minute, Antonio's arms are around my waist; the next, I'm dancing with Juan.

Let's do la Lambada, someone says.

No, siree. No lambada for me, I say.

Next thing I know, I'm sandwiched between two of them, dancing to Lambada. All innocent fun. A little dry humping won't kill anyone. I adapt to their language at my own expense. Except my inner alarm bells are ringing in my ears. Danger, danger, danger. I turn the music up to quieten my fight-or-flight reflex, my inner voice carving, slicing, sculpting, exploding— danger, danger, danger. I ignore the red flags stabbing at my gut. I drink, dance, and smoke on command. Maybe I kiss one, maybe two, maybe all of them in a cocktail of tongues. I don't know. Maybe I don't kiss anyone, they keep their private thoughts private, and we simply get stupid drunk. One helluva night.

The next day, the afternoon sun wakes me up. I'm curled up in a ball, the right side of my body numb from hours on the hard floor. Someone must have removed my running shoes but left my socks on. Someone must have covered me with a jacket. Maybe I looked cold in my tracksuit, and one of the boys lent me his coat. I instinctively pat myself up and down as if checking for missing body parts. It's all there. One of my buddies shakes his head as he inches his way out of the stupor. Brother! He exclaims, holding his head between his hands. The other friend is snoring placidly, his hand tucked under the waistband of his trousers.

I'm not shaking hands with that fucker, the other says.

I stay in the same position trying to make sense of last night. I imagine the scene from above.

A woman getting hammered with three freeloaders.

A young woman slow dancing with one inebriated man—his hard-on standing between them.

Two drunks dry humping a fresh-out-of-college girl.

All consensual.

Had anything happened last night, what would I tell the police? Would they believe that a group of best friends who came to the victim's apartment and drank her aguardiente at her behest would collude to assault her? C'mon now, it's the twenty-first century. A woman can have a good time with her buddies without being raped. Had anything happened last night, would I be calling the police?

I know the answer.

Betraying myself is easier than betraying my buddies.

Mercifully, nothing happened. I'm ashamed for doubting my friends' integrity, but I can't forget the alarm bells ringing in my ears. There was a definite moment when I was fully aware of my own vulnerability, when I realized that I wasn't just having a few with three friends alone but also with their body parts, three penises, and six strong hands. For a split second, I knew that if they decided to act on their lust, I'd have no defense against their army. Yet I paid no heed to the alarm system I was born with. I have been trained to be one of the boys. When shit happens, you take one for the team and move on. You don't rain on the boys' parade. In college, that attitude would have been social suicide.

I'm not in college. I'm a professional. I have a life, bills to pay, meetings to attend, an apartment to furnish, and a broken heart. I'm an adult. I got this, I say in my head, disgusted by the burn in the carpet, for which I'm sure the landlord will charge me an exorbitant amount.

I make my way to the bathroom, where I find the third buddy. He spent the night on the tiled floor after puking in the sink, the shower, the walls. I turn on my heel and head to the kitchen instead. My friends slowly wake up while I make black coffee. They clean up, and we reconvene in the center of the living room, sipping our coffees in silence, feeling shivery and hungover.

It's only Saturday, one of them says. What should we do?

They don't have any money to do anything or go anywhere. This is my chance to announce that the party is over, but, hey, I'm a good sport. We opt for the cheapest plan: more aguardiente and takeout. Surprisingly, out of the four of us, I'm the only one fit to walk to the nearest supermarket to buy more alcohol. Unsurprisingly, since I'm the only one earning a salary, it's understood that alcohol and food are on me. I reek of aguardiente and look like a woman with a problem as I walk down the street, shielding my face from the offensive sun with a quivering hand. I use the overdraft on my credit card to buy a bottle of aguardiente, and a roasted chicken, which I know won't be enough for the four of us, but it's all I can afford.

On my way back to the apartment, I identify a car amid the oncoming traffic. My English lover is behind the wheel, destination unknown. My mind goes mushy with a mixture of fresh heartache, drunkenness, and hangover, and before I know it, I'm leaving the bag with the goodies on the curb; I'm dodging cars, crossing the four-lane road to catch him before he passes me by. *I'm here, I'm here. I exist.* But my mad rush and the traffic lights are out of sync, and I jump right in front of his moving car as the lights change to red. I make him slam the brakes; I hear tires screeching, people gasping, and a few expletives hurled into the air. So much action takes place in a fraction of a second, I can't explain why or how I'm here on all fours flanked by my ex-lover's car, looking at my torn sweatpants, blood trickling from my scraped knees. The night before hits me with all its aguardiente-fueled force. I'm drunk again. I look up, and all I see is his 6'2" frame towering over me, his deep blue eyes eclipsing the sun. *Stupid woman*, he says, and goes back into his car. He slams the door with a fury that's a mixture of hatred and disgust. I get up as the traffic starts moving again, dust myself off, and walk as straight as I can across the street, a futile attempt at dignity. There is no sign of the bottle of alcohol or the chicken. Fuck me. Someone has stolen my bag. I start to cry in tiny, choppy sobs that grow in frequency and intensity all the way until I get home.

I don't want the boys to see the loser I know I am. I wipe my tears before I open the door and think of a good lie. I tell my disappointed buddies that the supermarket was closed. Either they believe me or opt for saying nothing about the booze in a gesture of camaraderie.

What happened to your knee?

Nada.

Really?

Nada, I repeat, and start to cry again, this time harder than a few minutes earlier. I'm gasping, crying, heaving, hurting. My face is a mess of snot, tears, and street grit.

They get up and offer me their arms.

No, I say. No.

Juan holds my hand and gives it a little squeeze. I don't know the meaning of that squeeze. I'm caught in a fit of cognitive vertigo, and his body language is incomprehensible. I let go of his hand.

I smell their breath. My buddies are still drunk, and my heart, my soul, screams at me, *Kick them out. The party's over.* I don't want their arms. I don't want their lust, jokes, words of comfort—sincere, or not. I don't want their friendship. I don't want anything. But, I'm so lonely that if they want a kiss, I might give it to them and then some. Pepe tells me that I look adorable with snot dripping out of my nose. I force a smile.

That sonofabitch doesn't deserve you, Antonio says, and puts his arm around my shoulder. I wriggle my way out of it.

Their presence begins to suffocate me. I need to be alone, but I don't have the heart or the courage to ask them to leave. I lean on a wall, my right foot close to the carpet burn, my left knee throbbing with pain, trickles of blood running down both shins. My buddies talk about the rest of the day while I study their feet. Cracked heels, toenails in desperate need of a good clipping, a sock with a hole where the big toe ends. How did I end up here? How do I stop from spiraling down? If life hurts this much at twenty-six years of age, how will I possibly make it to thirty? I consider not making it and immediately discard the idea.

The walls close in on me. I'm breathless, hungover, and angry at the Englishman, my buddies, myself, and the bastard who stole my chicken. I start to perspire heavily. I don't want to pass out in front of my guests. I go to my bedroom and lock the door. I lay on the floor where I sleep, cover myself with a tattered blanket, and the world goes silent.

I wake up on Sunday.

My buddies are gone.

I calculate the distance between the edge of my body and the popcorn ceiling, between everything within my reach and all outside. Unfathomable. The air in my room reeks of alcohol, nicotine, and failure; the world around me on the brink of implosion. My body is hungover, but my mind is stone-cold sober. I need to do something meaningful, something life-changing, something that causes waves and fires up volcanoes. But what? And, more importantly, how can I build a life while unraveling? I pull the blanket over my head, a simple move that uncovers my toes. The blanket's size sums up my life, and before I know it, I'm sobbing hard. I promise myself to let the Englishman go, buy a bed, decent sheets, and save enough for my own car. I promise never again to put myself in the vulnerable position I was in over the weekend. I promise to feed my body, stop smoking, and lay off the booze. I promise to listen to my internal alarm system and honor the signals my gut sends. I promise that if there is a next time, I'll say no from the start, and if my no goes unheeded, I'll shove, push, scream, kick, and scratch.

It'll take me months, years, and decades to fulfill my promises, but I don't know this yet. All I know right now is that Sunday mornings are eerily quiet in Bogotá, that the telephone hasn't rung in weeks, it's beginning to rain, and the walls of my empty apartment are silently closing in on me.

7

Milk, Oil, and a Night of Tequila

I smiled as the little Cessna flew over the central Andean range in Colombia. The Magdalena River snaked just below the belly of the plane, and it dawned on me that, from the air, its murky waters were nowhere near as beautiful as the pictures in the geography textbooks of my childhood. I caught my reflection in the window of the plane: a skinny girl with crooked teeth and frizzy hair on her way to her first field assignment as a drilling engineer. My smile grew bigger when the pilot announced that we were about to touch down in Barrancabermeja, the oil capital of Colombia. A short drive from the airport was El Centro, one of the oldest oil fields in the country. Qué Felicidad, oh joy.

At the end of the tarmac was the jeep with the company logo, waiting for me. I pulled my jeans down so that they weren't too tight around my narrow hips, lifted my suitcase, heavy with manuals and floppy disks, and walked to the vehicle. In my mind, the walk felt more like a levitation trick: I was high on dreams made of oil.

"Who are you?" The driver wanted to know.

"I'm the new engineer," I said.

He lifted his baseball cap to give me a better look, scratched his head, and scrunched his eyes as if trying to figure something out. "Oh boy," he said, before turning the ignition.

On our way to the rig site, he kept looking at me in his rearview mirror, grinning, as if the sight of me amused him immensely. One hour later, he parked the jeep outside two derelict trailers sitting on a patch of dirt across the exploratory oil well and handed me a package.

"What's this?" I asked.

"Two overalls size L, a pair of steel-toe boots size forty, and an adjustable helmet but," he made a small circle with his right index, "I'm sure it won't shrink to the size of your tiny head."

If his comment was meant to be an insult, it was lost on me because, compared to the circumference of the helmet, my head did look freakishly small. So what if I wasn't going to be able to wear any of it? If I could endure being the only girl in the classroom during seven grueling years of college, surely I could adjust the hem of my overalls with a stapler, stuff the toes of my boots with toilet paper, or fasten a helmet around my head. I was too proud of myself for making it to the oilfield to worry about these minute details.

I expected the driver to walk me to my trailer and introduce me to my boss, but he stayed behind the wheel, the ignition running. "We're here," he said as he lit a cigarette. I decided that from that moment on, I was on my own. He popped the trunk open, and as I took my suitcase out, he shouted: "They asked for an engineer, and the company sent a little girl. Unbelievable." I thought of a clever comeback but drew a blank. I was determined to be the toughest woman engineer to have set foot on the rig site. I would not complain, I would not cry, and I would not give anyone a reason to send me back to the office. Seré una roca, I'll be a rock. I had been given a chance to prove them wrong in their assumptions about women in the field, and I wasn't going to be a smart mouth on my first day.

"I hope you're ready, kiddo," the driver said as I waved him goodbye. "It's a jungle out there."

Perfect, I thought. I'm an Amazon.

He shakes my hand, introduces himself, and falls silent as he examines my body. His eyes linger around my wedding band, then my crotch. He is the field supervisor and will be my mentor and boss for the next three months. He pulls a toothpick from behind his ear, licks the length of it as he orbits around me, examining my body back and front, and tucks it behind the other ear. I don't know what to do. I stand in the middle of the trailer, trying not to move, as if immobility were the same as invisibility, and look at him over my shoulder, casually, like I haven't even noticed he is here. But he is. The Hotshot at the rig site, with his rugged face and the stubby three-day beard, the thick curly eyelashes, broad shoulders, and his cowboy-walks-in-a-bar gait, steel-toe boots, helmet and all. I'm sure he has slept with every available girl in the nearest village. I bet he hasn't forced himself on any of them; he is the kind of man that every girl would like to be seen with. Except me, a twenty-two-year-old petroleum engineer, married for two years to an alcoholic, and mother of a five-month-old baby. A naive woman who has spent the previous four months behind an office desk begging everyone in the oil company for a three-month field post.

Warning number one: he expected a guy, so no special sleeping arrangements were made. I'll have to share the trailer with him. Yes, of course, the bunk bed too. Top or bottom? He asks and licks his lips. *Desgraciado.*

Warning number two: a local girl from the village will come every weekend to have our uniforms washed, but my underwear I'll have to wash in the sink. I can hang my panties to dry next to his boxers on the towel holder. Silky thongs will be highly appreciated. *Pendejo.*

Warning number three: this is a war zone. If leftist guerrillas were to descend from the mountains onto the rig, no one would protect me. No special treatment on account of being a woman. He is all about equality. Ha ha. *Guache.*

Warning number four: the crews are made of rough men, pure riffraff. They won't treat me like a princess because, first, I'm not one, and second, because they have never seen a princess in their lives. They are uncouth. He is the only gentleman around. Ha. *Comemierda.*

Warning number five: he's well-endowed and knows how to use every inch of his boa constrictor. He is a light sleeper and has roaming hands. He is stealthy; I could very well one day wake up with the boa inside me. Just kidding. Or not. *Hijueputa.*

Warning number six: boys will be boys. That's the way it is; that's the way it will always be. If I have a problem with this, or if I go squealing to the bosses in the city, he'll send my ass back to the office and will make sure I never see a rig site again. He is my first real boss, but if I don't play my cards right, he'll be my last one.

It was 1989, Madonna's "Like a Prayer" had been on the Colombia Billboard Hot 100 for weeks, the oil industry was a man's world, and the notion of harassment in the workplace hadn't made it into our national dialogue. In fact, sexual harassment of women was inconsequential, a type of behavior not only perceived by men and women as the norm, but also encouraged among men. The bosses didn't send women to the oil fields. We were considered a liability. We menstruate; the rig site has no place for blood and tampons and sanitary napkins and cramps. Who wants an engineer with PMS? Women can get raped by any local lowlife, kidnapped by guerrillas, and get pregnant. No. It was much safer to send men. To let them do the harassing, the groping, the catcalling. To let them mess around with everything that moved. To let them be the lowlifes. For their actions, there were no consequences. And the big plus: men never get pregnant.

I close my eyes and think of his warnings. How can a man get away with this? What does the impunity of his actions say about the industry, society, country, and the world I live in? I know this: if I want to be accepted in the oil industry, if I want to earn the respect of my male colleagues in the field, I need to toughen up. But I'm not willing to pay for gender equality with my body. I cry quietly. I don't want to wake him up and let him see how terrified I am. The truth is, I can handle the harassment, the sexual innuendos, and the offensive stories I hear day in and day out here. But I'm afraid of being overpowered by a crew member as I walk around the site, of being sexually assaulted by my own boss. My state of alertness is such that I climb onto the top of this bunk bed every night, ready for battle. I won't go down without a fight. I leave my bra on, wear my two pajama sets, wrap the blanket tightly around my body, and carefully turn on my belly, trying not to loosen the wrapping. My hands at the ready, balled into tight fists. The moment I look at him through the space that separates my mattress from the wall of the trailer, I feel stupid. From the top of the bunk bed, he looks like a little boy. His right hand inside his boxers, the left tucked under his head, mouth halfway open, the bottom of his pearly teeth showing, and a little frown sits between his delineated eyebrows. He's got a perfect tan, square jaws, and fleshy lips.

Es un papito. He is a good-looking man.

He is an asshole.

I can resist all I want. Ignore him, act like a schoolgirl guarding her virginity on prom night, or play the good Catholic wife card. He makes himself clear: I'll be his appetizer, main course and dessert. It's a matter of time. If not today, I can be assured, maybe tomorrow or the day after. I will not be able to escape him. He says this and gives me a slow wink and a devious smile, half flirtatious, half predatory. We are at the tool-pusher's trailer-cum-office getting ready for our morning meeting. While the others arrive, I walk around the office and stop to examine the diagram of the blowout preventer valves on one of our well-heads. He stands behind me and whispers in my ear: "Have you ever seen a blowout? I'll show you a real one if you want me to." I recoil, move to the other side, and try to focus on a specific geological fault I find on a seismic line. He stands behind me, places his hand flat on the wall, and his bicep brushes my ear. I can feel his hot breath in my hair. I study his strong venous hands, his muscular sunburned arms and try to ascertain how much strength he would need to pin me to my bunk bed.

Not much, I'm sure.

Mi mamá answers the phone. She wants to know how I'm doing. I tell her it's fantastic. The rig site is like college, but instead of professors, I have experienced oilers competing among themselves to mentor me. Am I being respected? Am I being treated like a lady? Of course, I tell her. It's like they have adopted me. I'm somewhere between their little pet and their little sister to the young ones or daughter to the old ones. She wants to know if I'm eating well. I tell her about lobster days and steak nights, which is the only part of my rant that's true. Do I feel safe? Is it nice? Am I sleeping well? Do I have some privacy? I tell her, yes, everything is much better than I have ever imagined. I hear my baby laughing in the background. Does she miss me? I ask my mom. Is she eating well? Is she sleeping through the night? My mother tells me not to worry about my daughter. Between her and my sister, my baby girl is spoiled rotten. She has put on weight. She no longer looks like a preemie.

"Put her on the phone, please. I want to talk to her." I hear noises in the background. The TV is on; my daughter is watching cartoons. I hear mom's steps, the rustle of toys being moved out of the way, then my daughter's breathing into the receiver.

"Hola, mi amor, hello, sweetie," I coo into the speaker. "Soy tu mami. It's mommy. Are you being a good girl?" She starts to cry.

"I love you, sweetheart. I'll be home soon." She cries louder. Then we get disconnected.

We are having lunch under a tree. We would normally have lunch at the canteen at the rig site, but today Hotshot has brought me to a group of antiquated oil pumps called Catalinas, where four technicians are working on repairs. We all sit on our helmets and eat in silence. It's noon, hot and humid. A cloud of mosquitos descends upon us, but nobody bothers to swat them. We are overcome by a jungle midday stupor. The guys are tired from physical work. I'm exhausted from following them around like a puppy dog, of pretending I'm okay with the way they treat me with equal amounts of condescension, raunch, and disinterest.

I bite into my apple when Hotshot starts. He points at me with his plastic fork and says he's never met a chick with so many issues and that for being difficult, by the end of my stint, he'll have me walking as if I had been horse riding across Colombia for months. A shroud of silence envelopes the six of us. I can't tell what's going through their minds, and this uncertainty makes me wonder if they are entertaining the idea or have simply lost interest in Hotshot's fantasy. My breathing gets quick and uneven. A wave of panic rushes over me. *Tengo miedo.*

I swallow a chunk of the apple, eyes on my boots, adrenaline rushing through my veins. I'm not having lunch out in the field with five colleagues. I'm having lunch with five penises and ten strong hands. I have no defense against this army. I can't think of them as just men. I think of body parts and disparate levels of strength. I'm 5'5", weigh a hundred pounds, and have a squeaky voice. I walk around the platform with a clipboard against my chest, partly because I take notes of everything I see—I want to be the best drilling engineer the rig site has seen—and because it covers the stains around my milk-producing breasts. The clipboard is my shield. The way I see it, these men in overalls and helmets, these husbands and fathers, these boyfriends and sons, are armed and dangerous; they could turn me into a bloody mess of fluids and screams and nadie, no one, would come to my rescue.

Tonight, I think of my baby girl. I want to smell her, bury my face in the nook of her neck, and inhale her whole. I conjure up the creases on the soles of her feet, the dimple on her chin, the tuft of jet-black hair covering her perfectly round head, her protruding belly button, and I wonder if I had made the right decision when I asked my mother to look after her for ninety days. If leaving one's child in someone else's care while pursuing professional goals is worth the heartache. I know she is awake right now because my breasts are bursting with milk. I can't call mom because the telephone is in the other trailer, and I don't want to wake up Hotshot to tell him that I miss my daughter. The liquid oozes out of my nipples. I squeeze them hard, force the milk out of me, and dry them out with the pillowcase. Tonight, I'm alone, miles away from the only human being for whom I feel a kind of love that's mighty and transparent, like a diamond. Tonight, I don't want to be anyone's prey; I don't want to be afraid, I don't want to be wrapped up like a mummy. Tonight, I want to forsake my dreams of professional success in favor of my baby girl's lips tightly fastened around my areolas. I need to feed her body so that she can feed me. Perdóname, mi niña. Forgive me, baby.

Things I learned in college:
If I wanted to survive in a man's world, I had to compromise my identity, and rather than being the feminist my mother taught me to be, the assertive woman who knows what she wants and goes for it, I had to become one of the guys. There was no one on the whole campus with a filthier mouth than mine. My repertoire of dirty jokes was limitless. I spoke sarcasm fluently,

and the speed at which my tongue could spew mean comebacks was legendary. On field trips, I visited whorehouses, exchanged stories with any available sex worker, and patiently waited for my classmates in the lobby. Oh, and I learned to hold my liquor. I could drink anyone under the table.

At around nine, in he walks with a bottle of José Cuervo.

"It's Friday," he says. "Let's get wasted."

I look him straight in the eye. "Sure," I say. "Why the hell not?"

We sit across the desk from each other. He clicks his plastic cup against mine. He toasts to something, and we both down our first shot.

Hotshot asks me if I like it rough.

I let out a loud sigh and shake my head. No. *Qué idiota.*

Hotshot smiles like he doesn't believe me. He wants to know if I have ever had a threesome.

I say nothing. Instead, I roll my eyes, scratch my neck, and stare at him.

If I'm game, he says, he can call the mud engineer. They have threesomes all the time with the local girls. I make a dramatic gagging noise. He finds the gesture funny because he thinks it's the other man I find repulsive.

We have another shot. He stares at my breasts and flicks his tongue. Oh, man, he says.

Hotshot pours more tequila into my plastic cup and bets me I won't last half an hour.

Quiero llorar. I want to cry. I want to punch Hotshot in the face. I want to gouge his eyes out and draw my rage with my fingernails on his face.

We have another shot, and he makes a move. He stands up, tries to make his way around the desk, stumbles, pretends he is just stretching his legs and sits down again.

Do I have a kinky side? He wants to know.

Mi pelo, my hair, I think, but say nothing. I shake my head and pour us another shot.

He caresses one of his nipples over his shirt and tells me to slow down. He doesn't want me drunk. He wants me to remember this night because it will be the best I'll ever have. I'm a lucky girl: he and his boa constrictor are here to show me a good time, he says, squeezing his crotch.

His eyes are bloodshot, and his words slurred. Está borracho.

I stand up, pour more tequila into our cups, drink mine, give him a refill. He puts his hand up. I call him peso pluma, lightweight. Pfft.

He scratches his head slowly, says something unintelligible and drinks his shot reluctantly.

The tequila mellows me out. I sashay my way to the kitchen, where the cassette player is. I put on an old Cat Stevens cassette and press play. He sings "I'm Looking for a Hard-Headed Woman." I turn around and, emboldened by tequila, ask Hotshot if he likes hard-headed women like me.

He says: oh yes.

I say: come get me then, knowing that he won't.

He can't stand up. And even now, reduced to the little man I always knew he was, he has the audacity to ask if I'd suck him. Sure, come over here. Cat Stevens sings in the background. I contemplate my options in life and inside this trailer, look at this pathetic man in front of me, and see how physically beautiful he is. He looks like a muscular Cat Stevens. For a moment, I wish he weren't in a position of power. I wish I didn't know who he was and maybe, just maybe, could test the prowess of his boa. I wish the circumstances were different, that he were a tad soberer and I a bit drunker and could ride him bareback like a Navajo on her bronco.

I ask him for more tequila.

He stares at his boots, chin resting on his chest, and sighs; the exhalation makes his cheeks flutter.

He calls me a drunken whore.

I call him an asshole.

I return to the desk, reach for the bottle and command him to drink. Drink up, asshole. Be a man, drink. Drink up.

I'm frantically looking for a different insult, a colorful abuse heavy with scorn, the kind that splinters hearts and reduces egos to ashes. But I'm buzzed, and my mind draws a blank. I squeeze his cheeks, forcing his mouth open, shove the bottle into the void, and watch him squirm. I have violent thoughts; I want to yield to all of them. One minute, I want to crack the bottle and push the broken glass down his throat, to make him swish the shards inside the cesspool behind his lips, force him to taste the iron tang of his own blood, and render useless his vocal cords so I'll never ever hear his catcalls again. The next minute, I want to ask him about his mother. Would you like your mother to go to bed every night fearing sexual assault? What would you do to the man constantly threatening your mother with rape? Would you squeeze your crotch and thrust your pelvis as you cheer, or would you cut his skin open and wander into his heart, wielding a machete? Tell me, Hotshot, what would you do if it were your own mother?

His head hangs heavily to the right, then forward. He looks dead. I like that.

I seize the moment and climb into my bunk bed as I keep an eye on this dormant threat. I wear two pajama sets, leave my bra on, and as I wrap my body in a white sheet, I pray that my daughter never has to face a night like this. I lie on my back for the first time since I arrived here and allow my mummified body to enjoy the petty luxury of facing the ceiling. Hotshot is not sleeping underneath my top bunk. Tonight is indeed a special night.

I take stock of my life and conclude that the end justifies the means. The end is professional fulfillment and the means are surviving Hotshot's aggressions. I lie still, afraid of undoing the wrapping, afraid of being vulnerable to an assault, afraid of waking up this beast placidly snoring two feet away from me—the drunken asshole with the dead boa constrictor.

I make plans for my daughter:

I'll collect mi niña from my mother's house, find a modest studio with terracotta walls, and a corner for a hammock.

I'll teach mi niña to say no, and she will learn to push and to shove.

I'll show her how to keep her voice steady, hold gazes, and not back down if she knows she's right.

I'll help her find her place in the world and let nothing or no one move her away.

Then, I make plans for myself:

I'll finish my assignment in the field and extract from Hotshot a report exalting my performance at the rig site.

I'll leave the oil industry not defeated but filled with clarity.

I'll learn the difference between compromise and surrender.

I will stop trying to be one of the guys.

I will be the only thing I can be: a single mom.

A woman.

And that will be more than enough.

8

My Heart Has Its Own Way of Remembering Medellín

I wanted him from the first day he walked into my classroom. He was my Physics IV professor during my sophomore year in college, where I was studying to become a petroleum engineer. He looked like Richard Clayderman—the French pianist so loved in Colombia in the '80s. He was thin, medium height, had a killer smile framed by dimples, and a little hunchback that made him look like he was cold all the time. He also had a peculiar way of clearing his forehead of any strands of hair with a hand dangling in front of his eyes, fingers curled under his blond, baby-thin hair, then a clean sweep to one side. Or back. Or wherever the wind would take it. He seemed untethered. And that's what attracted me the most to him. His brilliance, which bordered on madness, was tangible, so corporeal and robust that it felt like another person in the classroom. He would come late for class or sometimes didn't show up at all. He would give us random low or high grades depending on his mood, the weather, or the alignment of the planets. On one occasion, after getting a 0.1 on one test, he allowed me to retake it. Not only did he give me the same test which we had gone over a few times after the embarrassing F, but he failed me again with another 0.1.

He talked about Einstein, Newton, and Maxwell like they were the Rolling Stones, the most radical, hard-core, coolest thinkers ever, and he was their most loyal groupie. His baseball-inspired lessons on aerodynamics were legendary. In them, he would get into one of his unique batting stances and explain that whether one chooses an open, closed, or even stance, whether one stands straight up, or crouches down low, the feet need to create a strong base.

We would tell him: we don't play baseball around here, by which we meant Medellín. And he would say:

If you've never held a bat in your hands, you haven't lived.

In my mind's eye, he stands right in the middle of the class-room, rolls the sleeves of his shirt up, and sets his feet. He bites his lower lip, grabs his imaginary bat, aligns himself with an imaginary pitcher, bends his knees, grips the bat with his fingers, and raises his hands (no higher than shoulder level, he warned us) with the back elbow creating a straight line to the shoulder that's parallel to the ground, bat raised diagonally behind his head, then he swings. Some students look at one another, pass notes, roll their eyes; some others cheer him on, complicit in his fantasy. Nothing distracts him from the object's trajectory. He keeps his eyes on the pretend ball, commands the class to go to the window and do the same—much to everyone's confusion—Pay attention! he yells, and when the ball stops, he does a victory dance, laughing his signature hysterical laughter that sounds like crystal pebbles rolling on metal.

Then he gives us the assignment: calculate the speed of the ball.

In less than a month, I'll be getting married to one of my class-mates—a dubious ticket to freedom from my overbearing moth-er—the only way for a decent Colombian young woman to leave her house: married. The semester is over, and Professor Karles is no longer my teacher. I buy him a book of poems and take it to his office. My way of saying thank you for teaching me about waves and electromagnetism. I enter his office, bathed in youth and exuding pheromones because I'm twenty and engaged to an alcoholic, and this, as wrong and pathetic as it sounds, makes me feel womanly. He stares at me with his painfully blue eyes, throws the book on his desk, and commands me to approach him. I oblige. He grabs me by my shoulders and kisses me hard. I think of the French pianist and how unlike Richard Clayderman, with his cheesy smile and LP cover tenderness, this brutish man with his tongue in my mouth looks. I don't like the taste of his mouth, a soupçon of corroded iron and sour fruit.

I'm having a bit of fun. Flirting with a genius makes me feel smarter, even though I can't tell anyone because I'm getting married soon, and I don't want people to think I'm a slut. Naturally, when Professor Karles invites me to his house in Robledo, I say yes. Robledo is the largest comuna in Medellín, known for its Spanish-style houses with orchids hanging from balconies and streets lined with ancient acacia trees. Maybe if we kiss in private somewhere in Robledo without hiding in his office, his tongue will be less probing and taste better. Perhaps if we kiss on his turf, his mouth will be more charming, more Richard Clayderman-like, and less thuggish.

I should have suspected something was awry when the bus driver announced that this was as far as he would make it. The passengers were asked to disembark and reach their final destinations on foot. This is not the Robledo I knew. This is the "other Robledo," the proverbial dark side of the moon, a place that shows on maps, but only a few would dare to visit. But I'm holding hands with my professor, feeling cocky, and strutting my flat hips like I'm Carmen Miranda reincarnated, sans the fruit hat. We walk past graffiti of leftist propaganda. Past massive murals with the names and faces of fallen comrades. Past *Gringo Go Home* signs, and paintings of grenades, rifles, and people in balaclavas. Past mangled cats and skinny dogs. Past antigovernment slurs, *Abajo Gobierno Hijueputa*, down with the fucking government. The graffiti and billboards in this "other Robledo" shout back and forth as if in a prison yard brawl, declaring their allegiances. A few shady characters come out on their balconies as if someone had alerted them of my presence: a college kid walking uninvited in the most impoverished neighborhood in the Robledo District, whose homicide rate trends higher than in Medellín proper.

A scrawny dog limps into a house whose entire front has melted and where weeds are growing out of the windows. A man with a bottle of alcohol in his hand trails behind us across the street. William seems to know him. He looks back over his right shoulder and says playfully,

Okay, okay, I know you're there. What's up, man?

The mysterious man says nothing and closes in on us. William doesn't stop. He holds my hand tighter and whispers in the man's direction.

Qué pasa, hermano? We're good, right?

Our tail is all the wrong type of swagger, the kind that makes one want to knock on a stranger's house and call the police. He crosses the street, dragging one foot more than the other, leaning to the right, grabbing his crotch as if for reassurance, flashing an oversized T-shirt with a marijuana leaf across his chest. He has bad teeth, bad skin, bad hair. He looks like grim news and a bad weather forecast rolled into one.

Who's this? he asks, jerking his face in my direction.

She is a friend. A good friend.

The man takes two long strides and is now in front of us, facing us. He shoves a bottle of aguardiente in my face.

Take a swig, he commands.

I look at William. It's 10:00 a.m., are you kidding me? I say, but the man is unmoved, and he presses the lip of the bottle on my chin and commands me to drink.

Drink up, he says. Just do it. I take a long swig and give the bottle back to the man.

Drink again, he commands, and this time, he tilts the bottle into my mouth to let me know he will decide how long my swig will be this time. The man passes the bottle to William.

Your turn, he says.

My professor stands tall, chest out, fronting the man with all his genius badassery. Richard Clayderman is all bravado now, much better looking than the pussy on my mom's LP cover.

Nah, marica, too early for me, he says, pushing the bottle away from him.

The man is not interested. He presses the entire bottle against William's chest.

Drink or else.

William takes four swigs. And I'm sure of the number because the man walks away proclaiming that now we/William owe him six swigs. He has given us something; later, he will want something in return. At some point, he will demand payment for this unwanted gift.

We arrive at William's house, which is a misnomer for this sad efficiency apartment where everything is broken or about to break; a dining table precariously balances on three mismatched legs, one shorter than the others. One military-style cot, the metallic paint of its frame peeled off just like the walls. A derelict door separates a malfunctioning toilet from the bed. In one corner is a gas stove with caked-on residue and grease splatters piled around its burners. None of this turns me off. On the contrary, all this neglect seems the most befitting place for my genius. We go out on the balcony just for a few minutes because, you know, people around here don't like new faces. I step over a couple of rotten planks and watch him, as if in a trance, roll two cigarettes. He puffs rings of smoke in the air while I try not to choke on this unfiltered nicotine hitting my throat hard. I take in the surroundings: zinc roofs, dirty alleyways, and overgrown lawns littered with condoms, sanitary napkins, blunt wraps, abandoned toys, beer bottles, the lot. None of it fazes me. My naivete keeps me from realizing this is no-man's-land. That there is no public transport because the place is too dangerous for bus drivers and outsiders, that the elaborate graffiti, which must have taken weeks to finish, exists because the police would never enter la comuna. I am too stupid to realize that I'm an unwanted visitor in this little country with its own reign of terror and unwritten rules.

William sips his black coffee, places the chipped mug on the banister, and kisses me. His mouth is roasted Arabica. Much better than the first kiss in his office. He rolls the sleeves of his pink pirate shirt and shows me the needle marks on his arm. Do I still want to kiss him? Of course, I think. *What I want from you has nothing to do with what you do to your body.* His kisses grow in intensity. They are no longer Arabica but a definite Robusta, high in caffeine content. I'm fully awake and high on coffee breath when he gives it all to me. He is a drug addict. Every two weeks, when he receives his pay from the university, he cashes it in, puts the wad of money in his jacket pocket with corduroy elbow patches, and sits outside his dealer's house. He hangs his jacket from a tree branch in his dealer's front yard and shoots up, smokes, snorts, or all of the above until he has given the dealer his very last peso. Then he lives for the next payday to do it all over again. He uses words I've never heard before. Angel Dust on good days; Angel Dust and gasoline on less-affluent days. Cocoa Puffs and 8-ballers when he can splurge; a few lines of blow on a rainy day; sometimes, he shoots up before class to sharpen his senses; some others, he settles for good old Mary Jane and booze because they are almost legal. And this is why he can't see his son. This is why his wife kicked him out of the house a couple of years ago. This is why his brother, the other Karles professor of also physics at the university, doesn't talk to him. Because he destroys everything he touches. Because he has been cursed with the Shit-Touch. The counter Midas Touch.

Now you know, he says. Do you still want to hang out?

I shrug my shoulders. Sure.

I'll be married soon, prof. I don't care how you spend your salary or what you put up your nostrils, veins, lungs. I just want to kiss you and have a little fun.

The truth is, I'm not thinking about the present. I'm thinking, soon, I'll be someone's wife—no longer mommy's youngest girl. I'll live in our house under my own rules. Later, I will be a petroleum engineer earning my own money to buy whatever the hell I want. The future is all I'm thinking of as my professor looks for something inside my mouth with his tongue, now perfumed in café 100 por ciento Colombiano. Richard Clayderman tastes like coffee. Who knew?

Pilarica, "the other Robledo," doesn't scare me; it excites me. It is a place with a pulse, unlike the other sterilized Medellín I inhabit with its rules and its police and its mothers with their unreasonable curfews. This is why William and I go to a local disco at 7:00 p.m., so I can still meet my mother's 10:00 p.m. curfew.

It's a lights-out disco, William says, swinging his imaginary bat.

I don't really care where he is taking me, but I ask anyway. What do you mean lights out?

Out, out, he says, like this ball, and he gets into his baseball stance and hits the imaginary ball hard out of the window above his crumpled, still-warm bed.

He offers me an eye patch. *An eye patch.* According to him, this will help me adjust to the darkness more easily. So absurd. I decline his offer. We walk out of the house, holding hands. He laughs at everything, and before I know it, I'm also laughing at nothing in particular. It doesn't occur to me that he could be high. Or maybe we are giggling because he is wearing ridiculous-looking red glasses at night. Something to do with rod cells' ability to see only black and white and sensitivity in night vision circumstances. Something to do with photopigments, the chemicals in both rod and cone cells that are light-sensitive and convert what you see into a language that your brain can understand. Something to do with rhodopsin, a photopigment found in rod cells critical to night vision. None of which makes sense to me.

The place is pitch black, but my genius navigates this darkness like a blind man on his turf. Either that or the red glasses have something to do with his fluidity. Or maybe his blue eyes have infrared capabilities. If he tells me he can fly, I'll believe him. I walk behind him with my hands on his waist, bumping into chairs, tables, and other people. The speakers blast old salsa songs. I'm on severe sensorial overload. I can't see anything, but I hear the music, the world, and the people around me; I feel their bodies passing me by, pressed against mine as they navigate this black hole; I smell cigarettes, weed, sweat, life. I'm in heaven. William finds a couple of chairs, and we sit down with our backs against the wall. I don't know that the Lights Out Bar exists so that rival gangs can dance to the best salsa collection in town without identifying and killing each other. I don't know that backs against the wall is the only possible way to sit here, to avoid being stabbed from behind.

Bullets are noisy, William says; knives are not. And he lets out one of his maniac cackles.

Instinctively, I laugh with him.

Best night of my life.

Two weeks before I get married, I see my professor at a little café overlooking a canal over the Medellín River. The fun is over. He knows this is a goodbye and has brought me a book of poems. A send-off into my future life which, he warns me, I will regret.

Come with me to Santa Marta.

What? No. I'm getting married.

His voice takes on a pleading tone I didn't think him capable of producing.

I know a little island surrounded by the bluest Atlantic waters, he says, as he folds a napkin in two, then in four. You'll be happy there. He clears his throat. I mean, we could be happy.

I'm not sure where he is going with this. This thing without a name we have, we agreed from the beginning, was nothing. Just a brief distraction. A little break from reality. *And oh, by the way, you are still married.*

A homeless man walks past the coffee shop shouting: cuando uno se muere nada se lleva. "You can't take it with you when you die," which my professor deems a perfect dedicatory on the book he is gifting me. He signs the book, pushes it across the table in my direction, and laughs his untimely, hysterical laugh that I adore. When he is done, he clears his throat and continues.

Come with me, he says. I'll write books on physics; you can read or dance or do whatever the hell you want. He unfolds the napkin. Folds it again. You will never find a whiter beach in the world.

I shake my head at his absurd offer but also have to chuckle at my predicament: marry an alcoholic versus run away with a drug addict. I choose the former. I don't see William again. I get married, against everyone's advice, get pregnant, against my family's wishes, divorce my alcoholic husband—according to everyone's predictions, and two years after our goodbye in the coffee shop, I finally graduate as a petroleum engineer, against all odds.

He disappeared not only from my life but everybody's. Soon after my wedding, he simply didn't turn up to teach the physics class and that was it. Nobody heard anything from or about him for almost three years. Not even his brother, the professor, knew where he was. Then one day, in a very William fashion, he showed up at his office and reclaimed his position. The university welcomed him back with open arms. No questions asked. When this happened, I was living in Bogotá, the capital of Colombia, where I was working for an oil multinational. The next time I flew to visit my family in Medellín, I went to my alma mater to pay my ex-professor a visit.

I want him to meet my two-year-old girl. I give her a white rose and instruct her to give it to the man with spectacularly blue eyes and a devastatingly kind smile we are about to meet. I knock on the door, the same door I knocked on almost four years ago to give him my book of poetry.

Come in, he says.

My daughter, the white rose, and I walk in, stand in front of his desk, and wait for the fireworks, but the man sitting behind a mountain of books is not the same man I said goodbye to at the coffee shop. He has an old man's eyebrows: bushy, wild, gray. I don't remember him being this short, this subdued, this scrawny. His face and arms look leathery as if he had spent the previous years under the sun, and his voice, my God, his voice has taken on a low, grave tone of slow, calculated words, so different from his legendary genius ramblings.

Hi, he says. I was expecting you.

My daughter hands him the white rose. He looks into her dark, curious eyes, takes the rose, and places it over his desk ever so carefully, like the rose is a bomb he is about to diffuse.

I sit down with my daughter in my lap and try to look casual as I take in the surrounding chaos. His office was messy before, but this is closer to neglect than carefree genius. He moves his chair from behind the desk and sits next to us.

I'm writing a book, he says.

I don't want to know what kind of book he is writing. What I want to know is what the hell happened to him. Was it the drugs? Where has he been?

What's the book about?

The center, he says. Well, it's more complicated than that.

How so?

I'm actually writing about the center of the center.

Oh.

There is a mathematical way to define it. I'm very close to it. Very, very close, he says, narrowing the space between his index and thumb.

Oh.

I'm clean and sober. Have been for a long time, he says emotionlessly. As if his sobriety is a journey he has embarked on grudgingly. I don't even smoke.

That's wonderful, William. I'm so happy for you.

He hands my daughter a piece of paper and a pen. While she fills the paper with squiggles and shabby lines, he gives it all to me again. This time slowly. As if he had rehearsed this speech for a long time and wants an immaculate delivery.

After my wedding, he went to the island off the Santa Marta coast he had invited me to. He read religious texts and found his own version of God. He started to write about the center of things: himself, the earth, the cosmos. He found there is an algorithm that points humanity not to a proverbial navel, but to a mathematical point at the center of the center.

I think of useful things to say. *Congratulations. Impressive. I'm intrigued.* I say nothing.

And I waited for you, he says.

What do you mean? Why would you do that?

Every two weeks, a boat with supplies came to the island. Naturally, every two weeks, I expect to see you. It was a matter of time.

Naturally? That's crazy, William. I never intended to mislead you. I made it very clear that I was getting married, and that would be it.

But his wait has its own narrative with voice and tone. He enunciates his sentences slowly, and each word sounds calculated and heavy. Each sentence: a cannon and a boom. I want to stop him. Tell him that this is ridiculous, that I never promised anything more than the brief moments of fun we had together. I want to tell him I didn't love him.

I don't.

He continues. I dressed in white linen. I'm from the coast; you know how costeños like white linen, he says matter-of-factly. Imagine me, donning a white fedora, white shirt, and white linen rolled-up trousers, every two weeks, like a character out of *One Hundred Years of Solitude*.

I shake my head and start to tear up. My daughter is now drawing on the floor, talking to her imaginary friends, and I am grateful that she doesn't understand the emotional weight of the moment.

Stop it; this is crazy, I say.

He doesn't stop. The port was nothing to look at, but it had a bench, and I thought, well, she can't possibly miss a man dressed in white sitting on the only bench around. But you never came.

This is one of those gestalt moments in life that can be summed up in a few words: he went to an island, got sober, found God, discovered a way to define the center of the center mathematically, and waited for me on an Atlantic-soaked bench at a port of sunbaked wood planks. He is not blaming me for anything. He is not presenting this new self as the victim of some unrequited love soap opera script. He gives the facts as if his past were a simple physics equation.

We exchange phone numbers and promise to keep in touch, a promise I don't intend to honor. I lift my daughter from the floor, hold her tight against my chest, her black hair catching my tears as I say goodbye to William.

Six months later, he calls. He sounds excited, almost like his old self, and I wonder if he is using again. He would like to come and visit my daughter and me in Bogotá. Will I welcome him for a couple of days?

Of course, I say, of course. That'd be wonderful. Have paper and pen handy? I ask.

No need. Go ahead.

The addresses where I live are incredibly complicated. Trust me, you need to write this down.

It's okay; I'll memorize it.

No, you don't understand. Even taxi drivers can't figure out how the address system in my neighborhood works. Please write it down.

No, he says in a commanding tone of voice. I will not write it down.

I find his reaction childish but acquiesce and give him the convoluted string of directions to my small apartment I know he won't be able to remember.

I'll be there this Friday. Will call you from the bus terminal.

We hang up, and something close to trepidation envelopes me. What if my genius thinks this weekend is the life-changing forty-eight hours he dreamed of while on the island? I am a single mom working hard to stay afloat in the male-centered oil industry. I don't need, nor do I want, complications now.

Friday comes, and he doesn't show up. I feel both relieved and disappointed at the same time. I want to see him; I just don't want the mess that he always carries with him like a badge of honor. Maybe tomorrow, I think. But Saturday comes and goes William-less. On Sunday evening, I call him.

A woman answers the phone. No, nobody by the name of William lives there.

He called me from this number just two days ago, I protest.

He doesn't live here, she says, her voice now muffled, like she is cradling the receiving with her hands.

He gave me this number six months ago, I insist.

Don't call again, she says, and hangs up.

I chalk it up to a disgruntled lover. Maybe they lived together, and things went sour. Perhaps he went back to his old druggy life, deserted her, and she is erasing him from her life. I don't know. I keep on living and don't think of him for another couple of years, until a friend from college comes to visit me.

She is a civil engineer and a single mom like me. We have a few drinks and talk trash about our college flings and crushes. Who dated whom and who broke whose heart? She tells me about her divorce from the medical school student she had married, who is now not only a successful physician but also a deadbeat dad with zero parental instincts. She fills me in about a couple of activists we used to know who went missing after I graduated. A teacher who won national recognition for one thing or the other, and of course, William.

You know what happened, right? she asks.

No. What happened?

Oh my God, are you serious? You don't know?

We lock gazes, and before she says anything, I start to sob.

Ruth cups my hands in hers. He got killed, she says. Apparently, he lived up there in one of the comunas and was a consumed drug addict. Did you know that?

I nod. But that was a long time ago. He cleaned up.

No, no, she interrupts me. Rumor has it about six months ago, William fell off the wagon and started using again. Hard. Got tangled up with a bunch of bad people and got himself killed.

Killed? What do you mean killed?

Oh, no, you really don't know. Ruth hugs me, puts my head on her shoulder, and whispers in my ear that he had been shot. He owed bad people drug money, and someone broke into his apartment while he was asleep, put a pillow over his head, and shot him twice.

I imagine his blue eyes blown into oblivion, right into the center of the center. Shards of his genius smeared on those peeled-off walls I loved a few autumn afternoons a lifetime ago. One bullet straight into his brilliance, his brain splattered all over that pillow without a case where I lay my head once or twice, the other bullet into his beautiful Richard Clayderman's face.

And the aftermath, Ruth says as she grabs my shoulders and pulls me away, so she can look into my eyes while she tells me the aftermath.

Whoever killed him found his phone book, and every single traceable person in it was also killed.

I'm grief-stricken and dizzy. I don't understand the meaning of my friend's words.

They turned his place upside down like they were looking for his phone book. You can imagine the rest of the story, right?

No, I can't imagine anything. By now, I'm sobbing into my hands. My shoulders rise and sink like a rogue wave off the Santa Marta shore.

Did something happen at his funeral?

What funeral? Nobody knows where he was buried.

I can't comprehend her words. Why would no one from the university pay their last respects to this brilliant professor?

Baby, Ruth says, baby, they went after everyone in his phone book. Everyone with an address got a visit and a bullet. Every. Single. One.

Right now, the world is fuzzy, too indiscernible to understand that he had spared my life on the day he refused to write down my address. Right now, my ears ring with a high pitch buzz Ruth can't hear. Right now, I'm mourning hard, too hard to say thank you for not writing my address, thank you for not visiting me, thank you for that infuriating weekend you stood me up and left me and my daughter dressed and ready with the table set for three.

I drill Ruth for details she doesn't know. I want answers. I want the reasons for his killing to match my grief.

Did they catch the guy who killed him?

Ruth shakes her head, almost apologetically, like it is her fault that the killer wasn't caught.

You know what it's like in Medellín. Nobody sees anything. Nobody hears anything.

I know what Medellín is like; thanks to William, I even know its deaf-mute underbelly. Pilarica, the other Robledo, is a strange little self-governed nation ruled by gang hand signals, tattoos, and bloody rites of passage. It's a tiny country compartmentalized by invisible walls. Walk beyond this block and get shot. Cross that street and get raped. Move into the wrong house and be thrown into debt bondage for life. Badmouth someone and pay for it. Pledge an allegiance to protect your family and get your tongue cut off. There are no rights in Pilarica. Only wrongs.

Was it a disgruntled student unhappy with one of William's random 0.1 grades? Was it his dealer, whose front yard I imagine as an unkempt patch of shabby grass littered with blunt wrappers, sorrows, and cigarette butts? Was it the aguardiente man whose demands as payment for the six swigs we forcibly took were too high to be met? Who could possibly hate him this much?

Ruth tells me they killed him on Halloween night, and the weight of the irony crushes me. I imagine his obituary. University professor killed in his sleep by a vampire. William Karles, a man of forty, killed execution-style by Goofy. The Universidad Nacional denounces the death of its faculty member, William Karles, who died at the hands of Captain America.

What was the world doing when my genius took his last breath? In the United States, the Halloween blizzard, a large storm system over the Atlantic Ocean, also known as the Perfect Storm, was punishing the eastern half of the country. Parts of Minnesota, Wisconsin, and Iowa were crippled by the large ice storm and record low temperatures. Between the blizzard and the ice storm, twenty-two people were killed. William was not one of them.

The English-speaking world couldn't get enough of Nirvana's manifesto "Smells like Teen Spirit." Do drugs, kill, lose.

Kurt Cobain killed himself twenty-eight months after William was executed.

Los Angeles is a ticking bomb after Rodney King's beating. The four officers accused of police brutality are being tried. The night William was killed, the officers' freedom was a strong possibility. Later, they were acquitted.

Cesar Gaviria, the Colombian president, sat to negotiate peace with M-19-guerrilla. We were tired of the violence. If we went on like this, killing one another, the left, the right, and the center, there would be no one left to write our bloody history. The day that William was killed, we, as a nation, sat down to haggle with the rebels over something neither party was willing to do: honor the truce.

The newspapers say nothing. William was one of twenty-four professors killed in that year. They were killed because they educated people, or because they had leftist ideas, or were drug users, or owed money, or talked to the wrong person, or were seeing here, or were overheard there, or took four swigs of aguardiente one morning in rotten Pilarica.

Last Christmas, my family and I visited La Comuna 13, District 13. Three decades ago, this was considered the most dangerous area in Medellín, a city deemed, in the '80s and '90s, the most dangerous metropolis in the world. Now, it's a very different story. Over the past years, La Comuna 13 has undergone a complete transformation, and the area is no longer known for gang violence, police raids, cartels, sicarios on motorbikes, and drug trafficking. They are still a community of casual workers, peddlers without benefits or pension plans, blue-collar workers with calloused hands and long commutes. Their houses are still precariously built and when it rains the muddy water runs as wild and ravaging down the steep slopes as it did decades ago. Yet, it's a different place. The district reinvented itself without demolitions or the erection of new and better buildings. Instead, hope filled and overflowed the void left by violence. The only gentrified part of La Comuna 13 is its soul.

Last Christmas, thirty-three years after the last time I walked these streets with my genius during our reckless sorties across invisible walls and enemy gang turfs, I walked them again. This time, I was holding hands with my husband of twenty plus years, a Scottish man who wouldn't have been able to visit the District a few decades ago. Behind me was my daughter, now thirty-two, and her Filipino husband. None of them had ever set foot here. My daughter grew up in the USA. I have lived abroad most of my adult life. And so we walked the District like foreigners, taking in the heartbreaking views of the city, enjoying the street performances, deciphering the encoded messages of hope encrypted in the larger-than-life graffiti dressing complete blocks. Every wall is a canvas. Every raiser in a staircase a poem, an act of remembrance, a self-affirmation quote. So much life.

The tour guide explained to us, graffiti is actually illegal in Medellín. If an artist wants to paint a mural, she or he needs first to obtain permission from the area's chief artists as well as the building's owners. I thought about telling my husband and daughter that it hasn't always been like that. That back in the day, the graffiti was the voice of the people living in the underbelly of

Medellín. But that wouldn't be true. The truth is way too complicated. So I kept that to myself.

Last Christmas, I realized that my heart has its own way of remembering Medellín and the past. I remembered the winding streets and their dark passageways with vivid clarity. I must have been here at some point. Yet, I couldn't remember any particular street or a specific passageway. Maybe I never had set foot here before. Maybe in my mind, every place on the outskirts of Medellín, where salsa music is a national anthem, and people with cigarettes dangling out of their mouths watch one another from derelict balconies, is Pilarica.

Last Christmas, we sat on the curb, and while savoring a soursop lollipop, I nearly told my daughter that once upon a time in this very place or a place very similar to this, there was a brilliant man who had, unbeknownst to me until it was too late, loved me. No, not just loved me. Who had gone to an island to get clean and waited for me so that I could bear witness and say, this man wrote a book about the center of the center. I was there. It was him. And he was a genius. But I'm sure she would have asked questions for which I wouldn't have had satisfying answers. So I kept that to myself too.

Last Christmas, as we came down from La Communa using one of the six outdoor escalators, I spotted a man who looked like William. An impossibility, as I don't really remember what he looked like. If he were alive, he would be a seventy-year-old man now. He would probably look as old as he did the last time I saw him in his office, bushy eyebrows, sun wrinkles, and thinning hair even though he was in his late thirties. What I'm trying to say is that last Christmas, as we came down the escalator, I spotted a man who looked like Richard Clayderman. Recently, I looked up the French pianist, now sixty-six, and, looking at his no longer angelical face, I realized with great sadness that I'm not sure if they ever looked alike. I remember body parts. Time, space, and distance have dismembered my genius. I remember his hair. Amber paper lantern. His eyes. Sapphires in the rough. His arms. The sand of that island off Santa Marta. I remember his impetuous lips. His feet in baseball stance. His curled fingers swiping his hair off the forehead. But not the whole of him. My professor's physical body has disappeared from my memory bank. Sometimes, when I think of William, I conjure up images of Aidan Quinn in *Desperately Seeking Susan*, his piercing blue eyes, that killer smile of his, and just when I'm convinced that William looked like him, my mind betrays me. I go back to the French pianist.

Last Christmas, I found myself scanning the tourists in la comuna, looking for someone resembling my genius. I found many white, tender-looking, blue-eyed, blond, mostly American young men. None of them looked like him. Or Aidan Quinn or the French pianist. As we got in the car and drove away, I turned around to see la comuna disappear behind me and wondered: Would Clayderman have held hands with a silly young girl who thought a premarital fling with a drug addict was a shortcut to adulthood? Almost certainly not.

And this is probably why

he

is

still

alive.

9

Silence: Twenty-One Variations

Inspired by Barbara Hurd's "Loneliness: Fourteen Variations"

1. At Six a.m.

On a quiet morning, I miss my daughter, my siblings, my friend on the other side of the Atlantic, my dead dogs, and my long-deceased mother. I miss who he and I used to be; the illusion of love from a stranger paying for my wine at a bar many years ago. I miss my cousin Karime and my maternal grandmother. I walk barefoot around the house, and there is silence in every room. The washing machine is off; the coffee maker flashes its silent light: brewing completed. The neighbors next door moved out, taking their daily piano sonatas with them.

2. In Front of the Mirror

The silence of my mornings has a mind of its own. Sometimes it's a cruel tyrant—the creak of my knees as I climb the stairs. Sometimes it's a mean Andean wind, and I wear wool socks and a Colombian poncho. Sometimes it's a mirror dangling in front of me, and I feel foxy in my fifties; crow's feet, my facial testimonies of a life well-lived. On days like this, I give my reflection a nod and smile of approval. Sometimes it comes with clairvoyant qualities, and I can see everybody's tomorrow and sometimes their yesterday with frightening clarity. Sometimes I wonder if there is something wrong with my silence. If it is something I need to fight off, avoid, break into pieces, transform into shapes, and fill with color. But most of the time, silence gives me something close to rapture. Its vacuum is a sacred moment, and in its void, I am divine.

3. The Silence

The Silence, an oil painting by the English painter Carel Weight, depicts three people observing the two minutes' silence on Remembrance Sunday. At the center of the painting is an older woman sitting in a wooden chair. To her right stands an adult man wearing a khaki jacket, black trousers, and brown shoes; to her left stands a blond schoolboy in uniform. There is nothing truly remarkable about this painting other than the silence, so palpable and present that it feels like a fourth person on the canvas. The artist, whose work revolved around human isolation, explained that he always found this silence very eerie, those moments when everything went quiet except for pedestrian sounds like a dog barking. *The Silence*, he explained, was his attempt at conveying his belief that although people join to perform identical rituals, they are essentially solitary individuals. To emphasize this, the three figures never met and were painted separately.

4. The Silence That Counts

The silence that counts keeps a score. On the rare occasion when I leave the house, the street noises confuse me. The traffic lights yell at me instead of flashing, and other car horns seem personal attacks on my character. On weekends, children trot and skip their way to the swimming pool, the playground where they mix their shrills in a cacophony of life that makes me want to hide under the couch. I know a woman whose high-pitched voice distracts me so much that I can never recall what she says. There are workers next door fixing the house for future tenants. The dull sound of their drills makes it across our thin walls, encroaches on my space, invades my office, it stabs at my ears, beyond the gum, the tissue, the muscle, all the way into the back of my eyeballs, past the three layers protecting my brain. Their noise is too powerful an army for my small silence.

Today, silence is waving its white flag.

5. The Noises I Can't Suppress

I have always thought of myself as a quiet-natured woman. That's not so. Quiet is a misnomer. I have a rowdy body.

When I meditate, I can hear my blood passing through the jugular vein and carotid artery. It makes a loud whoosh sound behind my ears, which I am always immensely grateful to hear. Sometimes at night, after the AC has dried up my nostrils, I hear a whistling noise inside my nose. An obstruction in airflow, a deviated septum, a tear in the cartilage between the nostrils, and childhood nasal trauma remnants. My cochlea is erratic, conniving, temperamental. It sends phantom noise signals to the brain; it makes me, and only me, hear ringing, buzzing, clicking, hissing, humming noises, sometimes in one ear, sometimes in both. It comes and goes. My cochlea is a lunatic. When I eat ravenously, carelessly, immodestly, or quench my thirst with a cold beer, I swallow air that knows no boundaries, which escapes my stomach in loud burps, like an ancestral roar. The air inside my gut is an orchestra. Not a philharmonic but more like a middle school music class, a collision of timbres, a tribute to dissonance; if I'm hungry, it grumbles on an empty stomach; if I overeat, it makes an odd, gurgling sound as it moves through the digestive tract.

My gut wears its heart on its sleeve.

6. *4'33"*

In August 1952, the American experimental composer John Cage debuted a three-movement composition called *4'33"*. It was composed for any instrument or combination of instruments, and the score instructs performers not to play their instruments during the entire duration of the piece throughout the three movements. At its premiere at the Maverick Concert Hall in New York, pianist David Tudor started a stopwatch, sat down in front of the piano, closed the lid, and began a performance in which he never played a note.

John Cage's 4'33" has been demonized and glorified in equal measures. The pianist's refusal to play arouses a cacophony of responses on the part of the audience: whispers, throat clearings, bodies shifting their weight on creaky benches, the sound of breath being drawn and exhaled in disbelief or outrage, hearts beating fast, all of it producing a kind of collective musical creation. For many, the purpose of 4'33" was a deliberate provocation, an attempt to insult or get a reaction from the audience. For many, it was a kind of artistic prayer, a bit of Zen performance theater that opened the ears and allowed one to hear the world anew. To Cage, its composer, 4'33" is an act of enclosing environmental and unintended sounds in a moment of attention to open the mind to the fact that all sounds are music. It is, according to Cage, a new approach to listening, perhaps even a new understanding of music itself, a blurring of the conventional boundaries between art and life. How ballsy. To debut a piece that calls upon the audience members to remain obediently silent under unusual conditions. A better name for the composition could be: Shut up and Listen to Your Own Music for Four and a Half Minutes.

7. At a Party

When I'm at a party surrounded by strangers, I become acutely aware of my accented English. My tongue refrains from the boisterous roll of the letter "r" of my native Spanish, shies away from difficult diphthongs; it trips and entangles. I trade spoken language for gazes and smiles; my curls come to the rescue and keep my fingers busy. I find interesting things on the floor, the walls, the sky, and the garden. I'd much rather be outside, over there, in the other room where fewer people are ready to exhaust the night with fewer words. I often wonder if my smile is too meek or unnecessarily flirtatious; if my eye contact is a lasso thrown in the air with no bull in sight, a waste of energy, a misunderstood optical illusion. I am a ghost walking around somebody's party, avoiding people, desperately looking for things to say, and saying nothing.

8. Over the Kitchen Counter

Breakfast. Sometimes I'm so pleased with the quality of my breakfast that I want to tell someone else. I slice an avocado; its skin breaks under the knife's edge. I remove the pit, a disembowelment of sorts, and scoop its oily flesh from the darkness of its shell into the night of my mouth, cave to cave, until the last green bit is gone. My mother, who taught me the right way to eat a mango by making a little hole at the tip like a boiled egg, and squeezing its juicy contents straight into my mouth, is dead. I live eight hours ahead of my family. I imagine my sisters' bodies in the concavity of their spouses', their feet dangling on one side of the bed, pillow marks on their brown faces, a grimace here, a restless leg there. What are they dreaming about?

I consider, for a moment, waking them up. Do they remember the avocado tree in our grandparent's backyard? Do they eat their mangos the way mom taught us to? They'd be, first, worried to hear their telephones ring this late at night, second, annoyed at their little sister's lack of consideration. I give up on the idea and peel a banana. The counter looks like a war zone. A disemboweled avocado, a spent mango pit, a collapsed banana peel like a drunkard accordioned on the sidewalk. I throw it all in a plastic bag. There is a rustle as it falls into the garbage can, then a loud crumpling of the trash bag.

Then nothing.

9. The anechoic chamber

The word anechoic means non-reflective, non-echoing, or echo-free. An anechoic chamber is a cavernous soundproof chamber with twelve-inch-thick concrete and steel walls lined with insulating foam blocks engineered to absorb noise. They come in all shapes and sizes. From small cubicles the size of a microwave to ones as large as aircraft hangars. Their objective is not to create silence—an impossibility—but to build a soundless environment suitable for conducting acoustic research. The anechoic chambers establish level noises produced by loudspeakers, military machinery, weapons, HiFi audio gear, vehicles, amplifiers, etc. This extreme quiet is eerie and otherworldly. People report feeling strangely uncomfortable inside the chambers. Sometimes, all they hear are their own heartbeats. For context:

A jet taking off produces around 140 decibels.

Babies can cry at around 110 decibels.

Typical car horns are approximately 108 decibels.

An opera singer usually is around 100 decibels.

Normal conversation around 60 decibels.

A whisper around 25 decibels.

Leaves rustling around 20 decibels.

Brownian motion (the random motion of air particles in space) around –23 decibels.

With a sound level of –20.6 decibels, Microsoft's anechoic chamber holds the Guinness record for "World's Quietest Place."

10. The Absence That Could Have Been Avoided

I check her Facebook page when I haven't heard from a friend in a while—because I didn't reply to her text messages or didn't pick up when she phoned me. There she is, looking into the camera, red lipstick framing her smile, hair in the air, blue skies above, green Gulf waters behind, and I think, why am I not there? Or sometimes, a few friends appear together, their arms thrown around one another's shoulders, their sororal faces beaming with tipsy joy, and I kick myself because I could've been there, broken my chrysalis and been a part of something beyond the walls of my house. Not finding myself in their moments makes me feel juvenile and clingy. I want to turn back time, barge into the club, the bar, the restaurant, the backyard, the beach dressed the part, a glass of wine in hand, sorry I'm late, got stuck in traffic, and pretend I never said no, insist they save a place for me in their lives, or at least dismiss me soundly enough to justify my next "would love to join you, but can't, sorry."

11. The Aftertaste of Bitterness

The silence after a fallout. The steely absence of his voice. The calculated reluctance to fill the expanse of our home with kindness. I walk into the kitchen, looking for traces of his love. The stove is off, and so is he. The more I think about the cause of the fallout, the smaller it becomes. It's over. I'm done with the silence. I want him, magically, to see the same smallness I see, to be as exhausted by our collective silence as I am, to slip back into my life without explanatory arguments. I send him a clear sign of a truce. I announce without fanfare that I'll be taking a hot bath. I sink into the hot water and wait for him to join in. By the time the water gets cold, I'm still in the bathtub waiting and shivering. I come out wrapped in nothing but a towel and high hopes. He has gone out for a bike ride. Reconciliation is a two-way street.

12. Vipassana

Silence has always been easy for me. Vipassana, a Sanskrit word that means to see things the way they are, is one of India's most ancient meditation techniques. Participants taking vipassana courses stay silent for ten days. They do not utter a word, refrain from making gestures or facial expressions, and commit to spending ten to twelve hours meditating, taking a few breaks throughout the day. When I was in my twenties, I did a weekend vipassana course. It wasn't anywhere near as hard as I was told.

Neuroscientists who have analyzed meditators' brains to see the impact of vipassana have learned that meditation strengthens the brain by reinforcing the connections between brain cells, a phenomenon called gyrification—the so-called folding of the cerebral cortex—which, in turn, may allow the brain to process information faster. Scientists believe that gyrification is responsible for making the brain better at processing information, making decisions, forming memories, and improving attention. Neuroscientists who have used MRIs to peek into meditators' brains have concluded that meditation causes the brain to undergo physical changes such as cortical thickness, which translates into lower heart rate and decreased sensitivity to pain.

13. Mozart's Silence

I listen only to the first movement of the Tragic Symphony. Its allegro con brio sends electrical currents down my nape. Sometimes I play it around noon, the quietest hour in my community. I turn the volume up and let the Mannheim Rocket bounce off the walls. A rapidly rising series of broken chord notes sparks out of the speaker. Mozart's twenty-fifth symphony has texture, is angry, and bursts the bounds of sedated classical music. What could have possibly made a seventeen-year-old so angry? The symphony opens with something close to a cry—the prelude to a hailstorm. His little G-minor symphony's first movement is tense, and terse, marked by fierce syncopations, pregnant silences, and a powerful bass line. I can't help it. I flail my arms in the air; my phantom baton draws drunken circles and wobbly number eights in the air. I'm a possessed conductor. I tremble and jolt with each incandescent violin. This is how I break my silence. I embody Sturm und Drang—the Storm and Stress, a moribund morning brought to life by sudden changes in tempo and dynamics, a private moment intoxicated with tonal extremes. I close my eyes and think of thunder, lightning, fire, destruction. Sweat runs down my back and the sides of my face. I nudge the orchestra to give me more, everything, surrender yourselves to me, I command. I rewind to seven minutes, thirty-five seconds, before the andante kills the buzz. I play the allegro con brio again and again. By the time my husband arrives, I'm disheveled and breathless, needing an exorcism.

14. During Sex

We leave the lights on so we can watch and bear witness to this process of heat, implosion, death, and rebirth. We are quiet lovers. The only noisy parts of our bodies are our tongues. They dart in and out of each other's mouths, and my body heeds the call; it unfurls, buds, readies itself to become something new. The blood vessels dilate. Increased blood supply causes a slow-motion swell down there. Fluid passes through walls. I'm porous and slippery. Everything south of the waist is swollen and wet. Something inside of me, small and secret, expands and begins to pulsate.

We use hands and legs to take each other hostage; we become barnacles, lock gazes—his impossibly blue irises on my brown eyes, and our pelvises do a furious dance. My brain turns into mush. It thinks in simple words. Yes, yes, right there, don't move, like this, oh, yes. My heart rate and breathing quicken, blood pressure increases; floaters are under my eyelids. His mouth sets my neck ablaze. I feel, at first, pleasantly hot, then unbearably flushed. I want him, a curious guest in my house, all the way in, exploring each corner of me, every opening with fingers, tongues, rigid body parts.

How can I describe him in the dark? I could tell you about the perfect roundness of his cranium, his thin savvy lips. I could tell you about the scar on his belly and the wiry texture of the hair on his chest. I could tell you that he is solid, manly, an expert in my desires. But what good are these descriptions in the dark? Better to say that we are ravaging each other in silence, that we are not talkative lovers. Better to say that he knows how to drive me to the end of my lust, that my desire for him feels animal, primeval, and tender all in equal measures. Better to say that we dance well together to Cage's *4'33"*, that by the end of its third movement, my body is pulsating a wet spasm. Better to say that we have woven a cocoon of metrical pleasure that my body trembles for fifteen, maybe twenty seconds to a soundless syncopation. How can so much happen in so little time? How can my body contract, expand, swell, shrink, and pulsate in complete silence? How can my mind fall into this psychedelic void of space and time without a shrill? When the major earthquake is over and I'm shaken by exquisite after tremors, we disentangle our bodies. His hands are his, and my legs are mine. Again. A different kind of whole.

15. Thich Quang Duc

Saigon, June 11, 1963. Buddhist monks gathered at a main intersection in downtown Saigon to protest the repressive practices of the Catholic Diệm regime that controlled the South Vietnamese government at the time. The monks wanted to make the world aware of the religious crisis in their region. They hinted at whoever cared to listen that they would pull off something spectacular by way of protest—and that would most likely be a disembowelment of one of the monks or an immolation. Once they reached the agreed gathering point, the monks formed a circle. Thich Quang Duc, a seventy-three-year-old monk, walked to the center of the ring and sat in meditation pose. Two young monks brought up a plastic jerry can filled with gasoline and poured it all over the older monk. He got a matchbook, lit it, and dropped it in his lap. Thich Quang Duc was immediately engulfed in flames. He remained in the same position. He didn't flail his arms. He didn't try to escape the flames. He didn't yell out in pain. His face stayed calm until the end. He died without uttering a sound. Pictures of his self-immolation remained as some of the most publicized pleas for religious freedom in history.

16. The Language That Hurts

Silence makes my jaw lethargic. I only realize how inactive it has been, how little extra effort my tongue has made for days or weeks when I meet with friends. After a few minutes of interaction, the temporomandibular joint, where the lower jaw meets the skull, becomes tender. Sometimes I try to visualize the movement of my tongue inside my mouth. The tongue's arch to the roof of the mouth for the high vowels of Spanish heard in the "i" of "machine" or "u" of "rule." The low, flat, and away from the palate position for the low vowels of English—"a" of "had." Maybe it's all the tongue acrobatics as I switch back and forth between my native and second languages that makes my jaw hurt. Maybe my prolonged periods of silence have nothing to do with the mandibular ache.

17. Ada's Silence

In the movie *The Piano*, Holly Hunter plays Ada McGrath, a Scottish pianist who has been mute since childhood. After being sold into marriage to a local man named Stewart, played by Sam Neill, she arrives on a New Zealand beach. She suffers torment and loss when Stewart sells her piano to George, a Maori neighbor with tribal tattoos across his face, played by Harvey Keitel. Ada learns from George that she may earn back her piano by giving him piano lessons, but only with certain conditions. At first, Ada despises George, but slowly their relationship is transformed. This propels a torrid love affair, a betrayal, losing a finger, a near-drowning, an escape, and the chance of redemption. In the closing scene, as she imagines herself in a watery grave alongside her beloved piano, she whispers, "It is a weird lullaby, and so it is mine. There is a silence where hath been no sound, there is a silence where no sound may be, in the cold grave, under the deep deep sea."

18. Nothing to Say (Pablo Neruda's Ode to Silence)

> *Now we will count to twelve*
> *and we will all keep still.*

Once, I was his sun. I was the raison d'être of her heliocentric universe. Their bodies were mine, and mine theirs. We grew intertwined. It was impossible to delineate my ends from her beginnings, to discriminate my jagged edges from the shadows of his soul—a triphthong of colors and tongue cadences. At last, a multicultural family, the coveted Trinity, with a dog, a house on the lake, piano recitals, sleepovers, and swimming meets. Then, one morning, one hundred ibuprofen taken in a spate of teenage angst upended the illusion.

∿

We held our breaths and walked into the hospital—a family in distress. Her entrails convulsed in orange pangs. I cried, prayed, pleaded. The powers that be were unmoved; she was Baker Acted. As the ambulance took her away from me, he held me in his arms, stunned, with nothing to offer but his warmth. Seventy-two hours later, we walked out of the institution. No longer a family. He, a stepfather; she, a stepdaughter. Between them, nothing solid enough to claim that the blood of the covenant is thicker than the water of the womb. We drove home in silence.

Each keeping their private thoughts private. And this is how she became. This is how he disappeared, how I dissolved.

Now I'll count up to twelve
and you keep quiet and I will go.

19. My Favorite Whistler

My mother possessed a splendid Helmholtz resonator in her mouth. We didn't know the fluid mechanics of her powerful whistling, nor did we ever imagine her oral cavity as a resonant chamber, but I am sure the lights in the houses of my childhood flickered every time she whistled. To her children, her mouth was for kisses and reprimands, not for music making. In *The Theory of Sound*, Lord Rayleigh described how the disruption of jet flow produces the whistling sound through a narrow aperture, something he called the hole-tone mechanism, which requires a resonant cavity and two nonvibrating orifices. Lord Rayleigh didn't weigh in on the despair of the whistler. He didn't consider that maybe the frequencies generated by hungry, disgruntled, melancholic, filled-with-unrequited-love whistles belong in the lachrymose sound category. When my mother whistled, she howled. When my mother whistled, the women in her bloodline heeded her call; they descended from the Andes to our tenement and held us all in their arms. When my mother whistled, my father's lovers could hear her war cry across rivers and jungles and they had to hold their breath, hands firmly planted on their chests, and they didn't breathe again until my mother unpuckered her lips.

Whistles resist degradation and can be intelligible at a distance ten times greater than shouted speech.

When my mother died, my sisters chose an ossuary in the basement of a church. I volunteered to deposit the urn containing her ashes in the crypt. It was a Sunday, and a chill came over me like a shroud. I wanted to put Mom under my sweater, sit with her on the floor of the ossuary, blow hot air onto the box, cover it with my hair, and sing to it. I wanted to shield her from cold and perpetual solitude. I couldn't bear the thought of condemning mom, the eternal whistler, the music lover, the loud disciplinarian, to eternal silence.

"Let her go," one of my sisters said.

I pressed the box against my belly, rubbed it on my chest as close to my heart as possible. Then I carried what was left of Mom to her new home. Holding my breath, I slipped the box into the crypt. With a steady hand, I pushed her away from this world and into her new realm. The box made a shhh sound as it slid out of my life and into the silent realm. I locked the ossuary, put the key into my sweater pocket, exhaled, and silently crossed that terrible threshold.

It was dark outside, and it was beginning to rain.

20. If It's Not What You Mean, Don't Say It

Q: What's the difference between a joke and a microaggression?

A: The size of the wound in the recipient's heart

B. The tone of the recipient's voice and the intensity of her frown

C. The distension of the recipient's jugular vein and the acerbity of her witty comeback

D. All of the above

As a woman of color in the twenty-first century, I am slowly learning that microaggressions require interventions, and these micro-interventions involve three strategies:

Make the invisible visible. If the perpetrator is unaware of the offense, speak up.

Educate the perpetrator: the impact of his words is heavier than his intention. Teach him the difference.

Disarm microaggression. If the remark sounds offensive and feels offensive, it is offensive. Speak up.

But I'm painfully slow to react and terrible at jumping to conclusions. Sometimes I hear a comment laden with vinegar and sand and fail to call it microaggression. I want to give the speaker the benefit of the doubt. I still believe in the spontaneous goodness of people and that not everything that comes out of their mouths follows a political agenda. I still believe that people sometimes say things they haven't thought through and that if they had taken the time to process their own thoughts before they became words, they wouldn't have spoken their minds. Some other times the malice of the speaker is plain to see, and I go numb. I doubt myself. Did I hear/read this? Did she/he actually say this? And if so, how am I supposed to react? What are the most effective, constructive, punch-to-the-gut words to remedy this ideological pathology? I'm learning the three strategies. I want to stop doing what I've done all my life: go quiet, play back the conversation, and ponder, sometimes for days, sometimes for months, sometimes for years. Silence, such an untrustworthy friend.

21. The Silence That Waits

The silence of a phone that never rings, a quiet inbox, a text message that never arrives. I am her mother. I'll wait.

10

Unfinished Business

It's 1983. Kenny Rogers and Sheena Easton have just released "We've Got Tonight," and I have secretly made it our song. We are outside the cinema holding hands and it's beginning to rain. A few minutes earlier, inside the movie theater, he kissed me so gently before the credits rolled, and I held my breath for fear of missing any parts of his mouth. When the lights were turned back on, we were still kissing with snarled tongues and crashing teeth. We've kissed many times before—on campus behind the engineering building, at the botanical garden under a majestic mango tree, in his house behind a door and away from his sisters' prying eyes—but the kissing today is different. His hands are bolder, like adventurous travelers, my fingers less timid, and the weight of our combined lusts makes each inhalation jagged, short, labored.

Lately, I've been thinking about the significance of my seventeen-year-old hymen and the implications of its existence. I want that half-moon membrane gone. I want it ripped, torn, sliced through with prodding male body parts and daggers burning in their sheaths. I want to lose my virginity with him and cross the invisible threshold that separates me from womanhood. I want to leave my adolescence behind, start a new life, and be born a warrior today under my sweet boy's weight.

He knows all of this. We've talked about it and we're ready. It's raining hard and neither of us has an umbrella. Before we make it to the bus stop, we pass the park where The Monument to Life sits. It's a colossal sculpture of a baby, a man, and a naked woman with fiery hair and a stalk of maize strategically located under her pubis, giving the sculpture a distinct air of weird sexual penetration. The only person around, a street fruit seller, closes her stall, plops the key in the side pocket of her blue jacket and disappears down the park, hopping over puddles of rain. Now, it's just the two of us. The raindrops get fatter with each passing minute; silver beads speckle our monument, drawing a curtain of wetness all around it. We look at the sculpture in silence and agree that this is the most beautiful place in the whole city. We are soaking wet and hungry for life. The kissing grows desperate, our mouths open and close like two fish flapping their gills on the road, both gasping for air. We stare at each other, our eyelashes heavy with rain, and I take a mental snapshot of this moment. He is a beautiful boy, and the arch of his beauty includes me. And so, we are flawless, young, and infinitely wise. Right now, I know everything there is to know about love. My boy double-dog dares me to take off my top and bra and run around the sculpture. I oblige, and he prizes my boldness with sloppy kisses when I finish running the circle. He licks off the puddles of rain formed in my ears, says something unintelligible, finds his way down to my breasts, flutters his tongue below my belly button, and at this point, my mind is gooey, my knees weak. All I want is to be teletransported to a quiet place where I can stop being a virgin.

We go to his house. We tiptoe our way to the second floor, still under construction, and amid bricks, bags of cement, and tools, we find an iron cot that he thinks his brother uses when he comes home drunk and doesn't want to wake up the family sleeping downstairs. We get to business quickly. We undress and kiss and caress. We stand naked in one corner of a dusty room with no electricity. The fading natural light reveals a pair of old Converse high tops under the cot, a plastic bag, an empty can of Coca-Cola, and an open pack of Marlboros. I bump my head against something hanging from the ceiling and my boy knocks down a wooden instrument that sounds like a guitar. Before I lay down, I remember having read in a magazine that guys like when women moan during sex. I do my best to moan through our heavy petting, to sound experienced. I whisper inaudible things and wait with bated breath for the thrust, the instantaneous passage into the rest of my life. My boy struggles, he is finding it hard to make his way into me. How many gates to paradise are there, for goodness' sake? How many tunnels from one country to the other? Sweet Baby Jesus. How could this possibly be so difficult? I'm here, ready, drowning in a pool of adolescent desire. C'mon, boy, make me a woman. But after a few failed tries, he says he is sorry, he doesn't know what he is doing. This is also his first time. He grabs his brother's guitar and starts to sing a song he composed for me. It's getting late. I need to start heading home if I don't want to miss my curfew. We are still naked, he is still singing bits of a broken song, and I interpret his musical preludes as disinterest. Let's do it, I urge him. He leans the guitar against the wall, helps me up, encircles my body with his arms and just when I think we are about to try again, he stops and says he's not in a hurry. He kisses my eyelids. We'll wait until the time is right. What's wrong with now? I want to know. Has he not seen the video of Kenny Rodgers looking into Sheena Easton's eyes as he urges her to find a way to make "it" happen tonight?

I start getting dressed. Scratch that. I start throwing my clothes back on. I feel cheated and the realization that it's cold and my clothes are still wet makes me even angrier. This walking away from his half-built room with my hymen intact was not what I signed up for. I was supposed to morph into a woman today. He offers to take me to the bus stop but I tell him not to bother. I can take care of myself. As I start to come downstairs, I hear his sad voice. Don't be mad, please, he begs. What's the rush? There is always tomorrow. I walk away and don't look back.

For the rest of the semester, we are still a couple but only on a kissing and holding-hands basis. We don't talk about what happened in his house or whether we will try it again. During finals, he gives me a notebook chock-full of poetic declarations of love of his own creation. Poetry doesn't deflower, *boy*. Before the end of the semester, he drops out of college and leaves without saying goodbye. And that was it. I never saw him again, the beautiful boy of strident laugh and unruly curls.

My unfinished business.

Many years later, I received a short letter from him. He had gotten my address from a mutual friend from our university years. There I was, married to a good man, raising a young daughter, getting giddy at the thought of him, the seventeen-year-old boy I once loved with all my adolescent fever. The moment I saw his writing, I began to feel submerged in a hazy nostalgia, a savage hunger for the past like no other. I conjured him up in bits. An open-mouth smile of even white teeth. His unapologetic laughter, always generous, a field of dry leaves in full rustle. Brown eyes that sparkled like children's in full rapture. A few curls peeking from beneath that heinous beanie hat he wore even if it was hot. I took my time to invoke the shape of his nose and the arch of his eyebrows; I did this meticulously as if nose and eyebrows were splendid artifacts from a long-lost civilization. In my mind, I traced the outline of his fleshy lips with my index finger, the lips of the boy I once loved. Other than a telephone number, he gave no personal information in his letter. So typical of him, I thought. Just hi, how are you, I hope you are well, bye—still a mystery to me even after all these years. I started to dial his number but stopped halfway. I had an old heart versus brain standoff. Please be single, my heart prayed. My brain, always the wiser of the two, begged: please be married. Very married. Have oodles of children. Be strangled by commitments.

I said hi, he said hi. And that was the gist of it. There was nothing remarkable about our first and only telephone conversation. He sounded detached, distracted, almost as if my call had caught him in the middle of something more important than hearing my voice. After a few awkward silences, one of us, I can't remember who, mentioned meeting in person, then one of us, I can't remember who either, mentioned a cup of coffee. Both said yes to a meeting in the botanical garden, the same place with the mango tree under which we had many long make-out sessions a lifetime ago.

A few days later, I took a shower and went to meet him with wet hair and not a dab of makeup. I wanted him to see the real me, the budding wrinkles around my eyes, the permanent frown like two stabbing marks, the little acne scars on my chin. Also, I braced myself for an unflattering older version of him. Maybe a man with a protruding belly, curls shaved off into an unattractive combover, nicotine-stained teeth, uneven fingernails, and patches of unkempt stubbles. In the taxi, on my way to the garden, I remembered his arms around my body, my face snuggled somewhere between his clavicles, and I wondered if he was now as tall as he was the last time he held me in his arms.

I arrived before he did. I reacquainted myself with this place I had loved in my youth. The garden was both different and unchanged. The place looked equal parts chic and primitive, with modern structures and architectural elements sprinkled over vast swaths of green. Yet, the smell of gardenias and ripe mangoes was the same. I felt young and lovely again. I yielded completely to the urge to take off my sandals and walk barefoot on the garden's grounds. As I walked around feeling the grass under my feet, it dawned on me that I had left his telephone number at home. There was no way to message him to let him know I was already there or for him to message me to tell me that he had gotten cold feet and he wouldn't come. I sat on a patch of freshly manicured grass by the gate and scanned every man who entered the garden. Too tall, too short, too young, too old. What did he really look like? I was getting nervous, unsure of what exactly the purpose of this meeting was, when I spotted him. He walked with long, ostrich-like, bouncy strides, both hands tucked in the front pockets of his jeans, and that open-mouth winning grin—his signature. He was taller than I remembered and had a splendid pair of firm legs which I didn't remember him having before. Instead of a combover, he had a thicket of loose curls, and where I expected to see a protruding belly, there was nothing but a simple shirt neatly tucked under his belt. I got up and waved in his direction. He waved back and kept walking toward me unhurriedly. Like an expensive stallion who never loses his cool. No, scratch that. Like a man with a lot of time to spare. No, like a blend of grapes and sugar, slowly fermenting, patiently transforming itself into the finest bottle of wine in the cellar. Before we even said hello, it crossed my mind that I would love to have a sip of that wine.

We hugged clumsily, kissed each other on the cheek, and held hands as we walked, looking for a bench to sit on. He smelled of peppermint. After he had dropped out of college, he moved to a different city—new beginnings and all—to study physics and mathematics. He had been a math teacher all these years. And in case I was wondering, no, he never got married—marriage was not for him—had no children, nor intended to be a father any time soon, and no, he didn't have a steady girlfriend either. I examined his face as he spoke. Oh, and in case I was curious, no, he wasn't gay. He was in an open relationship with a woman who shared his love for freedom. She visited him on his farm whenever she felt like it, spent however long they wanted to be together, then disappeared for weeks, sometimes months. I wanted to ask if he loved her. I didn't.

And there he was, a beautiful man in great shape who had never been inside a gym. Instead of kettlebells, he had worked on his farm for years growing everything that stuck, a trial and error type of thing because he didn't know anything about agriculture. The smallest job at the farm took him a long time because he had never owned a car; he had only driven motorbikes, and how much mulch can you carry on a bike, right? As he spoke, I imagined a parallel life with him. We live together on this farm overlooking the city. Our house is small and cozy, with a wall-to-wall fireplace in the living room. We don't have children, which means we are two free adults ready to take off at the smallest whim. We have two lusty dogs who escort us to the house with a cacophony of barks, yelps, and yips from the moment they spot our motorbike.

And me? He wanted to know about me. How could I tell him about my complicated love life, my globe-trotting adventures, the challenges of raising a girl with a mind of her own, all the nuances of my nomadic life, always on the move, always at the ready to leave it all behind? I opted for a simple version of my life: I have a daughter and a wonderful husband.

The sun started to set. The sky turned a violent shade of orange. A gust of warm wind made him blink. He had long, curly eyelashes. How could I have forgotten? Maybe it was the foreboding sunset announcing the closing of the garden, the end of our meeting, the impending and unavoidable goodbyes which made us nostalgic. By the time the horizon had devoured the sun, a primal melancholy was raining down on us, heavy and relentless, like hail.

He had his own recollections of our evening together; I had a truckload of mine. We had collusions and disagreements on a few details here and there, but the memory was clear, present, and so substantial that it felt as if it had happened the night before. From the Marianas of that night, he dredged up a specific memory of our sexual explorations. I had forgotten this, yet somehow, I mourned the loss of that sweet memory. For a few minutes, I allowed myself to be immersed in the realm of possibilities. I grew restless. The weight of what could have been became unbearable for me to carry alone. We talked about that afternoon in his house, filling in each other's blank spaces with such detail that it began to feel like a form of masturbation.

"Would you like to see the farm?"

"When? Now?"

"Yes, now."

We knew where this was heading. I was afraid of saying yes and of saying no. So, I didn't say anything. Instead, I sighed.

"My bike is parked around the corner."

"Oh, man, don't do this."

"We can take a cab. We'll be there in a jiff."

"It's getting late."

"What, you still have a curfew?"

"Kind of."

We ordered more coffee. Although he had never been married, he understood my predicament well. He talked about life from his bike: the hidden corners of this land he had stumbled upon down deserted bends; the rhythmic swoosh of the wind hitting his helmet when he rode on open roads; the young river with the colorful rocks he found by accident the day he lost control of his bike and ended up covered in mud and dazed on its V-shaped shores; the bed of four o'clocks he mistook for butterflies from his bike made him make a sharp U-turn, and when he realized they were flowers, not butterflies, he parked his motorcycle, zipped his jacket up, and stayed there by the road all night until the sun came up and the fuchsia trumpets closed down again just because he could.

The botanical garden closed. We were the last ones to leave. The last time he offered to take me to the bus station, I declined.

This night, so many years later, as we crossed the street to the taxi stand, he held my hand tightly, and I returned the squeeze without looking at him. We said goodbye, we hugged, we kissed on the cheek, but neither of us hailed a taxi down. We stood there, pinned to the ground, unable or unwilling to commit to anything other than this moment. He didn't ask to see me again. I didn't suggest keeping in touch. We knew that whatever was going to happen, it would have to be now, or the possibility would die.

"A taxi would take us to the farm in no time at all."

I closed my eyes. He cupped the back of my head with his hands until my forehead rested on his chest. My heart pumped hard inside my rib cage, and I felt dizzy, like the beginning of a weed-induced high, not unsteady or heavy, but a blur of happy arousal. My only guess is that he felt the same way. His body hardened, his heartbeat grew frantic, and before we caved in, we peeled ourselves away from each other. It was a solemn moment of recognition for what we could have been and respect for whom we had become. There was no epiphany, no scripted goodbye, no revelation. He hailed a taxi, I got in, closed the door, and looked at him through the window. He smiled wide, clearly the only smile he had ever mastered, tucked his hands in the front pockets of his jeans, and kicked some dirt with his right shoe. I could've opened the door, gone around the corner to wherever the hell he had his damned bike parked, and ridden pillion to the farm, wind in my hair, arms widespread to the elements, the protagonist of some corny soap. But I knew better than that. Goodbye.

I got in the taxi and didn't look back. From the backseat of the taxi, I imagined his silhouette against the incoming traffic, slowly drowning into a swift stream of headlights. I perfected that image in my head; I fondled the idea of him disappearing, becoming smaller and smaller in the distance, the warm memory of his firm body leaving my arms. It was as if he had been hallucinated into my life, magically grafted into reality in the ink of his letter. I closed my eyes and extricated him from my history, one remembered sloppy kiss at a time until I was irrevocably reinstated as the married woman I was before he found me. I took a long breath, and with it, I mustered all the courage I had to turn around and see him one last time.

He was gone.

11

Who Owns My Body When I'm Unconscious?

Truth be told, I don't need to be here. The "click" in my knee can be fixed with physiotherapy. The thing is, appointments with the physio won't take me away from work, which is what I desperately want: sick leave. The guy I've been dating at work has just ended our relationship, and I'm heartbroken. Well, that's a lie; we weren't dating. If saying I do at a cheesy chapel on the Las Vegas Strip counts as an actual marriage, we were married.

My knee started clicking while we were dating, but I was high on adrenaline, infatuation, pheromones, or witchcraft, and the pain was never intense enough for me to seek help. The pain was never sharp. That's a lie too. I'm exaggerating it because I need time off work to regroup, collect my thoughts, and see if, by some divine providence, I can continue working eight hours a day next to this man who doesn't want to be married to me. I'm also blowing the pain out of proportion, giving its physicality more space than it deserves, because my knee joint gets more attention than me. In the story that unfolds at the orthopedist's office, my knee is the protagonist, and through it, I get to enjoy thirty minutes of undivided attention vicariously.

The first time I came to see the orthopedist, he was seeing his patients an hour behind. The plastic surgeon at the clinic must have deemed this delay the perfect time to drop by and make his sales pitch among his colleague's patients. Well, not really. He chose me among the four or five people in the waiting room. First, he walked around in his immaculate white coat, examining each of us above the golden rim of his reading glasses. Someone must have asked who he was, because twice he pointed at his name tag lanyard with the clinic logo embossed to one side, then shook hands with a woman in crutches, and introduced himself to a man with his right arm in a cast. Pleasantries over, he stood tall in front of me, asked me if it was okay to sit down for a second, and before I could answer, he moved an empty chair to my right and sat next to me. He moved his head back and forth, analyzing my profile, and after complimenting my hair, I think, or maybe my eyes, I can't remember; he pointed out the only problem he could see with my face. It was a deviated septum, something that he could fix in a flash and make my face perfect because it was the *only thing* that wasn't perfect about me. Forgive my boldness, he added. I turned around to face him. Unless the deviated septum he wanted to fix was in my breasts, it was clear he was not interested in my nose. From then on, I avoided him like the plague, to no avail. He always seemed to know when my appointments with the orthopedist were, and whether I entered or exited through the front or back door.

One day, after the secretary called my name, I was walking down the white corridor leading to the orthopedist's office, passing other doctors' offices along the way, when the plastic surgeon appeared behind one of those closed doors. It had started to feel like he was stalking me. He acted happily, surprised to see me. I responded politely to his enthusiasm and walked a bit faster. So did he. Had I thought about the nose? He could fix it, outpatient, in and out. Perfect face in two weeks. What do you say? I said no, thank you, and walked off. At least, I think I walked, although it felt like I was sprinting away from him.

On a different occasion, I was halfway through the consultation with my doctor; my skirt bunched up mid-thigh when the plastic surgeon walked in announced. The interruption didn't surprise my doctor, who exchanged pleasantries with the surgeon while tweaking my knee this and that way. I should have said something, but I was a good Catholic girl who had learned not to cause unnecessary scenes, not to make too much noise, and not to turn a minor situation into a big drama. My doctor and I discussed options: a quick fix to get rid of the elongated cartilage in the surgery room, which would give me a month off work—what I wanted—or months of physiotherapy sessions and no time off. The plastic surgeon walked around the office, sat at the doctor's desk, opened a few cabinets, and closed them again. Do you share offices? I asked, afraid of sounding impolite. They looked at each other and exchanged a nod and a smile I recognized as complicit. They knew something I didn't. They colluded silently on something I couldn't discern. A secret male code that escaped me. Whatever it was, they were in this together, and I was a clueless variable in the equation. I breathed a sigh of relief when the plastic surgeon left just as unexpectedly as he had arrived. The respite lasted only a few minutes. Conveniently, he had a few questions for the receptionist at the same time I went to pay for my consultation and schedule my upcoming surgery. This time around, he put his arm around my shoulder, only it wasn't threatening enough for me to squirm out of it; it was a friendly doctor type of thing. Hey, what about your nose? I'll do it for free, just because you are such a pretty thing. Eh? I said no thank you, and, uninvited, he walked me to my beat-up Fiat-147 in eerie silence.

The divorce is finalized, and my heart aches more than my knee. A week later, sleep-deprived and emaciated from self-imposed starvation, I walk into the clinic for the wrong reason, ready to have the surgery I don't need. It's early in the morning, and I am the first patient. Mercifully, only the operating theater is open, and the doctors' offices are still closed. I go through the preparation process with no sight of the plastic surgeon. I sigh with relief as I get wheeled into the operating room. The mask is on, hair tucked in that ridiculous-looking paper hat, and IV ready to send me into oblivion. I realize I have revealed too much to my doctor during our appointments. Two weeks ago, while he checked the X-Rays and asked me about my life, I told him how lonely I am in Bogotá, a city so different from my beloved Medellín. My boyfriend/husband had recently dumped me. I'm bored at work. Life, simply put, sucks. He was receptive, kind, and nodded at my confessions as if he were thoroughly acquainted with loneliness. He listened to my woes like he had also been jilted at twenty-five and made a single parent by a partner unfit to be one.

I hear a woman's voice, the anesthetist, I think, asking me if I'm ready. I say yes. Let's get that knee fixed, shall we? my doctor asks. I nod, start counting back from twenty.

The lights go off.

When I wake up, I'm in the recovery room, naked under a thin sheet, trembling from cold and loneliness. That's not accurate. I feel lonely, but I'm not alone. Next to my bed stands a bespectacled eagle holding my bedsheet up in the air with its beak. I can't decide whether the bird of prey is about to go for the kill or about to fly away from a juicy young kill. I'm still groggy from the anesthesia; maybe I see things. I don't trust myself. The next time I open my eyes, instead of an eagle, I see a magician waving his white cape in front of his face, an impossibility as I am in a hospital. Scratch that. I close my eyes, rest, open them again, and the caped man's face comes into clear view. I soon realize he is not a magician but the plastic surgeon camping under a white tent. Wait a minute. He is not camping, and there is no tent. He is crouching under the hospital bedsheet covering my body.

How are you doing, sweetheart? he whispers, caressing my face with the back of his hand. You look delicious, even post-op.

I look at the clock and take a mental note of the time. It's 11:15 a.m. My right leg is bandaged from the ankle to my groin. I'm thirsty. My mouth is dry, and I can't say what I think. I want two things: to see my orthopedist or a female nurse, and this man out of my room.

Is it too tight? the surgeon asks, moving his hand under the sheet toward my leg.

I shake my head no, as vehemently as my drugged-up body can. I try to push him away, but my hand feels heavy with the IV needles and something clipped to my index. Tears roll from the corners of my eyes, forming a puddle in the bay of my ears.

You did great, sweetheart; you are so brave, honey, the plastic surgeon says.

He wipes my tears with his index finger, then licks it off. Suddenly, everything goes out of focus. I fall asleep again.

I have wondered for years why he was allowed in my room.

Where was my orthopedist, the nurses, anyone, when I woke up?

Had the plastic surgeon been allowed to be present during my surgery?

How long was I with him in the recovery room?

What did he do to me while I was unconscious? Did he look, or did he touch? Did he touch, or did he penetrate? Did he feel himself while looking at me? Did he masturbate while I was unconscious?

How many times had he done this to other patients?

After removing her tonsils or appendix, did a woman wake up to his prying eyes too, or was it just me?

Did the doctors have a secret agreement? Did they take turns violating their patients under anesthesia?

Were the female nurses part of this?

Did I imagine all of this?

But the real question, the kicker, the one I can't comprehend, is why I said nothing. I asked the nurses if anyone had been in my recovery room around 11:00 a.m. They answered no, I was recovering nicely, and they had left me to rest. No one would have believed me, I was convinced. A heartbroken, divorced, twenty-five-year-old single mom high on chemicals is not a reliable narrator. My life had already maxed up its quota of messiness. If I made waves, I could very well have drowned in them. Every young woman of my generation knew that.

What could I have said? I didn't have any proof. All I had were hazy memories of an eagle cum magician cum doctor. Of what could I have accused this man without evidence? How does one prove molestation? How can the unwanted hand on your belly, the undesired touch of the back of someone's hand on your face, and the lustful eyes scanning your naked body while semi-unconscious have any weight in court? Only thirty years after the fact, it dawned on me that I had sanctioned the surgeon's behavior with my silence, that my inaction had been translated into go ahead, do it to other women, count on my complicity.

We now have words we didn't have in Colombia in 1991 to describe what happened: sexual harassment, stalking, unethical behavior, medical malpractice, sexual abuse, abuse of power, negligence; the list goes on. Thinking about my younger self lying on that recovery bed makes me feel more powerless now than I did at twenty-five. No, that's another lie. I didn't feel powerless back then. I didn't know I had any power. How could I have felt the absence of something I didn't have? I don't know what this man did to my body. I will never know how far he went. If rape kits existed back then, I was unaware of their existence. How could I have asked for things I didn't know existed?

This was a long time ago—water under the bridge. I don't remember the names of the doctors or the clinic. But I remember the sunless sky hovering over Bogotá and the wintry wind hitting my face as I stepped into the parking lot looking for my beat-up car. I remember the crutches digging into the folds in my armpits. I remember shame so bitter I could almost taste it.

I juggled with my purse, the crutches, my shivering hand unable to put the key inside the lock, the jammed car door, the mini-breakdown I had with my head pressed against the side of my white car.

I don't remember how I unlocked the door or how I lowered myself into the driver's seat with my right leg in a cast. But I remember my fingers gripping the steering wheel. I screamed, hurled insults at no one in particular, disengaged the hand brake, turned the ignition, and stepped on the accelerator pedal, ignoring the sharp pain in my leg. I drove behind a screen of tears. I remember feeling desperately lonely and inexplicably dirty—as if it was me who had done something morally reproachable.

I can't remember if I got lost before or after it began to rain. But I remember the puddles in the street, the deafening sound of thunder, the black skies suddenly hit by flashes of lightning, and how small I felt beneath it all. I took the wrong turn and by the time I realized I was driving against traffic, it was too late. *So, this is how I die. Cars honking, pedestrians shouting expletives at me, drivers giving me the bird. I remember trying to make a U-turn but being unable to maneuver the clutch and the gas pedal with my right foot. This is how my story ends.*

I don't remember why I chose this particular man. But I remember parking at a bus stop, my sad-looking Fiat pointing in the wrong direction, much to the horror of the people hunkering under the shelter. I rolled the passenger's window down and shouted at this scruffy-looking man shaking his tatty umbrella in a high-pitched voice I didn't know I had. Can you please help me turn the car around? I asked him, lifting the crutches in the air for him to see. The stranger lowered himself to look inside the car. He must have seen the crutches, the stupid woman at the wheel, the tears, the quivering lips begging for help. He shook his head in disbelief, scratched his chin, and sneered. He must have thought, fuck me, as he stepped into the rain, skipped a pothole, and came to my rescue. I remember that he helped me out of the car, his hands uncomfortably close to my breasts as he adjusted the crutch pads under my arms. I remember thinking the man could very well drive away in my car, leaving me on crutches on the sidewalk. But he waited for the traffic to slow down, turned the car around, and came back.

I don't remember if I paid him or if he even wanted anything in exchange, but I remember his cigarette breath in my face as he said: Jesus, sweetheart, don't you have a man to drive you around?

I released the clutch slowly and pressed the accelerator pedal.

I don't need one.

Remember when I said water under the bridge? What else is there to say when you are young and lost, your mother has trained you to pee quietly, avoid confrontation, arrange your messy hair into two tight braids, be a good Catholic girl, and worship God and his representatives on earth: priests, doctors, and lawyers, in that order?

Fast forward twenty years. *Twenty.*

I'm on an examination table, trying my hardest to visualize the speculum. For some reason, understanding what goes on inside my body during a routine pap smear relaxes me. I want to work with it, be an obedient team member, and get this over with as soon as possible. The gynecologist pushes the tool deeper, and I squeeze my eyes shut instinctively. She tells me to breathe in, relax my lower abdomen; she is almost done. She pulls the speculum out, and before I sigh with relief, I feel her gloved index go into my anus. What are you doing? I protest. Oh, she says, we are now instructed to look for polyps at the same time. Her finger wriggles inside me in tiny circles. It probes the walls. It looks for something that's not there. I tell her I hate what she is doing. She doesn't acknowledge my discomfort or apologize for the well-meant intrusion. I question the ownership of my body. Whom does it belong to once I put the feet in the stirrups? Do I have a say in the speculum's size or which orifices get inspected?

She removes her gloves, disposes them into the "biochemical waste bin," and announces that I need to see the gynecologist for further examination.

Wait, you are not a gynecologist?

No, ma'am. The gynecologist no longer performs pap smears; we, the nurses, do.

I'm confused and feel slightly more violated now. I thought she was a doctor who specialized in women's bodies, but she is not.

You have an elongated uterus. Not a big deal, she says, but it's best if the gynecologist sees you.

A week later, I'm in the doctor's office conveniently located next door to the one where I had the pap smear. Two women are waiting to be seen, and I wonder if they know about the rectal examination. I'm tempted to tell them but decide it's none of my business.

The receptionist calls my name and escorts me to the oncologist's office. While I wait, I look at the doctor's credentials on the wall. A Doctor of Medicine from University X, a post-graduate degree in gynecology from University Y, and one in oncology from University Z. Why am I seeing an oncologist?

He is handsome, in his late thirties, I estimate, and very well respected—the best gynecologist in this part of Florida. We shake hands, and I'm momentarily struck by the blueness of his eyes and good looks. He reads my file and mumbles the words "elongated uterus," followed by a hmm and another hmm, a little nod, and a downward pull of the corners of his mouth like a bad omen. I go on the stirrups again. Mercifully, he doesn't do the rectal examination. He orders blood tests, an ultrasound, an MRI, a hormonal count, and the lot. I go home convinced that the tests are unnecessary. My body and I have an excellent relationship. I usually know when it needs tweaking, alignment, TLC. I know when there is something wrong. I won't try to explain it; I do. Plus, I won't allow anything to dampen the excitement of our upcoming cruise, a wedding anniversary gift from my best friend.

The results are in. My husband sits beside me in the doctor's office; I'm at ease, convinced that he has taken time off work for nothing. But he is jittery and holds my hand tight as the doctor examines the results clipped on the X-ray film viewer. The oncologist opens my file again, reads something from it, looks at the viewer, and I hear the same ominous hmm, hmm I heard during our previous consultation. He turns around to say something to us; his face looks like bad weather.

Do you see these two dark spots here? He asks, pointing with his pen at each side of my "elongated uterus."

My husband and I nod. And this is a moment when being a woman changes your understanding of the world. I've had ovarian cysts all my adult life. They come and go; that's what they do. Millions of women get them. Most of mine have vanished just as they have appeared, gradually and painlessly; a few have succumbed to birth control. But my husband doesn't see it that way. He nervously clears his throat at the sound of *two cysts, one in each ovary.* One the size of a tennis ball, the other the size of a ping-pong ball. He looks so alarmed that I feel compelled to tap his hand with mine reassuringly. It's okay, I whisper, but he is focused on the doctor's diagnosis.

If I were you, the handsome oncologist says, I'd have these bad boys removed immediately. I shake my head and assure the doctor that this is not new. I've dealt with these minor inconveniences in the past, and they have gone away.

Are you planning on having children in the near future? the doctor asks.

I force a polite smile.

I'm in my forties. Of course not.

My husband is not taking this lightly. What's going on? Why are we bringing children into the equation? my panicked husband wants to know.

The doctor is very nonchalant about it.

If you are not planning on having children, it would be in your wife's best interest if we take everything out. You know, to avoid future hassles.

And this is another moment when being a man changes how you see the world. This man, who has spent about twenty-five minutes of his life with me, suggests, casually, that I surrender my uterus and my two ovaries, the parts of me that make me who I am. Why is swift mutilation his weapon of choice? If I were a man with, say, gastritis, would he recommend that I have my testicles and my prostate removed, you know, to avoid future hassles? I'm mulling over things like agency and ethics and the Hippocratic oath when I hear my husband ask:

Could it be cancer? He doesn't sound like the assertive man I've known. He is scared. The doctor turns his back to us, studies the films from the sonogram, and does his thing again: hmmm, hmm, we'll know when we open up. I see endometriosis here and here and here, he says, tapping the film with his pen. I remain unfazed. Every woman in my family has endometriosis in varying degrees. My mom, sisters, and nieces suffered from terrible monthly pelvic pain. I'm the lucky one of the lot. My diagnosis at age twenty-five: asymptomatic endometriosis.

How long have you had that? my husband asks incredulously, like I'm revealing that I had an affair. If there is a possibility that you might have cancer, we need to schedule surgery, my worried and now very pale husband says.

I discuss a few things with the doctor. I don't want him to take out anything that doesn't need to be taken out. I'm very clear about my wishes. I agree to surgery that only removes the cysts if found cancerous or damaged beyond repair. He is to leave everything else the way he finds it. The doctor says he'll do his best but can't guarantee what he will discover once he opens me up.

The oncologist looks at something on the screen of his computer.

I have an opening next week, he says, after looking at his calendar.

No, I say firmly. My husband and I are going on an anniversary cruise next month. I'll schedule surgery when we come back.

He leans over his desk, positioning his stern face closer to ours.

If I were you, I wouldn't wait. I don't like the color of those two masses. A tennis ball, he says, making a capital C with his right hand. No, we can't ignore that one. A ping pong ball, he does a lowercase c, might be terrible news.

We schedule the surgery for the following week.

As soon as we return to the car, my husband breaks down. It's September. Hurricane season has been kind to Florida this year, and the sky is a deep blue. I bring him close to me over the handrest and let him cry in my chest as I admire the cloudless sky. Am I in denial? Why am I not worried? I'm more concerned about my inconsolable husband than the possibility of having cancer. I'm fine, I tell him. I don't feel anything. I would know if there was anything wrong with me. But the decision has been made. Next week, I'll find out if I have cancer.

A nurse gently taps my shoulder when I wake up from the surgery.

Wakey, wakey, sweetheart. Time to go home.

The nurse, the room, the IV, everything is out of focus. I squeeze my eyes shut, and when I open them again, my husband appears in clear view. His blue eyes are reassuring. He kisses my forehead and tells me that I can go home. Am I imagining this? I just woke up from general anesthesia and have been repeatedly asked to go home. I can't even keep my eyes open.

Wakey, wakey, missy, the nurse sternly repeats. If you don't open those pretty eyes of yours, you can't go home. You need to go for a walk.

I'm trying my hardest to open them, but the eyelids are heavy and unresponsive. I think I fall asleep again. I wake up to my husband towering over my bed, grabbing my chin, and moving my face gently from side to side.

Wake up, honey. You need to go for a walk.

I can't even remember what kind of surgery I just had. My body and mine are foggy. I don't understand why I need to go for a walk. I need to rest. I want to sleep. Maybe I'm having auditory hallucinations. My husband leans over me, puts his arms under my armpits, and helps me upright. The abdominal stabbing pain refreshes my memory. I just had two ovarian cysts removed. I sit on the edge of the hospital bed, but I don't have the strength to stand up. I think I fall asleep again with my head on my husband's chest.

Wakey, wakey, I hear the nurse say once more, her voice now less motherly and tinged with exasperation. Do you want to go home? she asks.

I say no, I'm tired, but she doesn't hear me.

You need to go for a walk.

Next thing I know, I'm walking down the hospital corridor, stooped over with pain, the IV pole turning its wheels by my side, my husband supporting me with one arm and the other closing the back of my hospital gown, his attempt at allowing me some dignity.

When I am fully awake at home, my husband shares the good news with me: the doctor didn't find cancer. I want to cry. I want to say to my husband that I knew it. I knew it. All this for nothing. I want to say I told you, but I don't. No cancer. That's the good news. The bad news is that the doctor had taken out my right ovary. Why? I want to know. My husband doesn't know why. He can't remember. All he remembers is that the doctor told him everything was fine when the surgery was over.

Does she have cancer? my husband remembers asking him. The doctor seemed shocked, as if my husband had asked him if he had found a pair of lost shoes in my uterus.

Cancer? Of course not. Why would she have cancer?

And the news he heard right then was all that mattered to him. He rejoiced. His wife didn't have cancer. How wonderful. How lucky. How blessed. Whatever else the doctor said, my husband doesn't remember well, only something about the right ovary, the one with the capital C tennis ball.

The days pass, and I hear nothing from his office. I don't receive the standard courtesy phone call to check on the patient. No one is wondering if I have an infection or if I'm in pain. I'm a closed file for them. Two weeks after the surgery, I call to schedule a follow-up appointment.

By now, the small laparoscopic incision is healing well, and although I should be happy at my speedy recovery, I can't shake the grief over having lost my ovary. On our way to the doctor's office, my husband slows down, coming almost to a complete halt before every speed bump. He doesn't quite understand why losing an ovary upsets me so much, but gets the physicality of a bounce on the road after abdominal surgery. He gets what's tangible, how driving over a speed bump magnifies the pain in a traumatized body. I can't ask him to understand that my body has been broken into, rummaged through, and raided. My ovary. I'm beginning to sound like a broken record. My ovary.

It's still September, but the stores are offering many Halloween trappings. Our little Floridian town is bursting with candy, costumes, pumpkins, fake tombstones, and bad wigs. We drive past Party City. A mannequin is dressed in an American Suffragette costume; she holds a sign that reads Give Women the Right to Vote. My ovary.

The doctor comes to greet us at the door of his office. His tan reveals a weekend in the sun. I wonder if it is from largemouth bass fishing in our local chain of lakes or hours on the golf course. He shakes hands with my husband, then me. We agree the weather is gorgeous and the traffic across town is a nightmare. He asks how we are; we say fine, thank you, and, as is customary, we ask, And you, how are you, doctor? Hear me out. Stay with me for a second here. How he answers this mundane question, his body language, and the tone of his voice make me wonder if I'm still a suffragist. He holds our gaze in silence, the expression of a jokester creating suspense before the punchline, claps his hands once, only once, then rubs them together vigorously before proclaiming:

A few more months like this one, you know, with back-to-back surgeries, and I should be able to retire in a couple of years.

I'm stunned and so inexplicably ashamed that I can't even look at my husband. I sit down and stare at the back of the doctor's computer as he reads what unfolded during my surgery.

Hmm, hmm. Endometriosis everywhere.

No kidding, genius, that's what endometriosis is: the appearance of endometrial tissue outside the uterus. He says it was best to remove the right ovary for the sake of my health, not the present but the future. Oh yeah, he adds, as if he had just stumbled upon some forgotten information. I also performed an appendectomy.

Did you take out my appendix? I asked, shocked by the news.

Yep. Trust me. It was covered in endometrial tissue. As I said, I found endometriosis all over.

Was anything sent to pathology? I ask, since the word cancer had been uttered before.

Pathology? He seems surprised that I even know the word. No, no need, he adds. You are very lucky.

My mind is awash with questions. Who owned my body in the operating room? When did I authorize this man to cut me open and remove my organs at will? Was my request to remove only the cyst and leave everything as he found it considered? How does endometrial tissue make its way out of the ovarian region and into the junction of the small and large intestines where the appendix lives? Where are my organs? Were they disposed of into the proverbial biochemical waste bin, or are they being used for research without my knowledge, as with Henrietta Lacks?

We drive home in silence. I think about asking my husband what he thinks about the doctor's early retirement at my expense. But I don't want to sound like a victim, although I feel like one. In my head, I rehash the question: *What do you think about those poor women who most likely have had healthy bits taken out in the spirit of not their present but future health?* It's a futile exercise. My thoughts don't translate themselves into words. I'm too drained, too grief-stricken, too humiliated to talk. As ludicrous as it may sound, I'm in mourning, yes, grieving over the loss of my ovary and now my appendix. When I get home, I lock myself in our bedroom and have a good cry. I feel abused, the borders of my skin trespassed, and trampled. Life goes on. My husband returns to work, and mid-October finds me spending hours researching at the computer. I want to understand what they did to my body.

The findings:

Adhesiolysis is the removal of the cyst along with its capsule and any remaining endometriotic foci.

However, small asymptomatic cysts should not be treated surgically, especially in patients older than thirty-five.

That's me, a woman over thirty-five with asymptomatic cysts. In such cases, medical literature deems surgical treatment unnecessary.

Unilateral oophorectomy while sparing the contralateral ovary is the most efficient preventive measure for recurrent ovarian endometriosis. That's the good news. The bad news is that such a procedure should be considered in women with another endometriotic cyst in the same ovary. This is not my case. I had a single cyst on my ovary. Again, according to medical literature, a unilateral oophorectomy should not be given much consideration. The other bad news is that surgical treatment is linked to the early onset of menopause since half of the ovarian reserve is removed by surgery. I repeat in my head the words "early" and "menopause." Why did the doctor not mention this before the surgery? That the procedure could potentially rob my body of another ten years of healthy hormonal life makes me angry, bereft, sad, all with the same intensity.

Parkinson's Disease, PD: Women who have had an oophorectomy are at increased risk for developing parkinsonism and Parkinson's disease later in life. Although the risk is higher—about double—for women with both ovaries removed, even removing one ovary may increase the risk. Why was I not told this? Why did the doctor, who specialized in women's bodies, fail to mention that should I lose an ovary during surgery, the subsequent drop in endogenous estrogen levels could turn my life into a mess of earthquakes and shakes?

I also find that although uterus-like masses frequently appear in the ovary, they rarely occur outside ovarian regions, so it would be extremely rare to find endometrial tissue adhered to the appendix. In such extraordinary cases, the woman would experience sharp right lower abdominal pain indistinguishable from acute appendicitis. I was fine when I went to have my annual pap smear. Nothing hurt. I was not in pain. A deep sense of helplessness washes over me. I'm defeated. I'll never get back my organs or the past few weeks of my life. The cruise was a non-refundable deal. We will not see the Bahamas anytime soon. When friends and family call to check on me, I give them a standard, I'm fine, thank you. I wish people would stop asking how the surgery went. I don't want to talk about this. Unfortunately, every time I eat, I develop a dull pain in my abdomen's upper right area, two inches to the right of my navel. I'm convinced that the pain is related to the surgery, and once again, I find myself shaking hands with the no-longer-so-handsome oncologist.

He makes his hmm, hmm noise, then tells me that maybe, *maybe*, my body formed a keloid scar where the appendix used to be.

He explains that sometimes a scar grows bigger and broader than the original injury. It has nothing to do with him or the procedure, he is quick to add.

It's genetic, he says. Yep, it runs in the family.

I want to throw his desk upside down, put my fists through walls, and leave a keloid scar on his tanned face. But he disarms me when he asks, Does anybody else in your family scar like this?

Yes, I say—all of us.

Bingo, he says.

There is his eureka moment. That little aha, told you, nothing to do with me. But to make sure, he wants to run a test, an eco-

one thing or the other, or maybe a sono something. He instructs me to tell his receptionist to schedule a test with a code that escapes me, but which, for the sake of the story, I'll call XYZ123. I walk out of his office, repeating in my head like a little girl, XYZ123, XYZ123. I stand beside the receptionist and ask her to schedule the test. I repeat the instruction but quickly realize she is entering the wrong combination of letters and numbers. I correct her, but she, very gingerly, explains there is no mistake.

Oh, the code? Don't worry about a thing. The insurance company pays better for this other code but, fear not, honey, you will get the proper test done.

We lock gazes. I'm disgusted; she is unfazed. She looks like the type of woman used to turning alpha into omega, water into a thick stew, and still gets what she is instructed to get, plus a bonus from her boss.

Never mind, I say. Cancel the test.

Oh, let me run it by the doctor.

I don't care what he says. I'm not having the test done.

I turn on my heels and drive home in a fit of fury. I could have made a scene, embarrassed the receptionist, the doctor, myself, and accomplished nothing. This health system is a complex machine whose parts function in mysterious ways. I go home and call the insurance company. I want to know what exactly they paid the doctor on top of my copay.

My file arrives a week later. The insurance company has been billed for three different procedures: an appendectomy, a unilateral oophorectomy, and a laparoscopy (to treat endometriosis). Each procedure has a listicle of items used during the three surgeries that range from surgical gloves, masks, and cotton balls to specialized/professional services.

I'm hunched over the kitchen counter, reading the travesty the treatment of my internal organs has become. I catch my reflection on the glass door of the microwave. This is me: an immigrant woman in her forties who left a beloved but messy third-world country when she was in her twenties in favor of an organized nation where immigrants' dreams of a better life come true. I see me: an educated, well-traveled, well-read immigrant woman trying to understand and failing at making sense of this country's health system. What happens to the bodies of other immigrant women when they seek medical attention? Those who don't speak English and can't explain where it hurts, those undocumented women afraid of being deported if they seek medical help and who die in their trailers of "unknown causes," those who don't know that their ovaries and appendixes were taken out unnecessarily, those whose bodies are used to make a doctor's dream of early retirement in the sun possible.

It's 9:00 a.m. in Florida. I sit in a high stool chair in the kitchen, debate whether it's too early for a G&T, and allow myself to imagine my ovary's fate for the last time. My imagination runs wild with all sorts of ovarian poetics. In a petri dish, used to save humanity, a personalized version of the HeLa cell line. Sinking languidly in the Atlantic Ocean, a lifeless jellyfish on its way to oblivion. But the real question, the kicker, the one I can't comprehend, is why I said nothing. Here I am, a woman with a voice, education, and access to resources remaining mum about an act of aggression against my body. I'm no longer a heartbroken, divorced, twenty-five-year-old single mom high on chemicals with a dubious narrative. Do I still operate under the assumption that if I make waves, I could very well drown in them? Every woman in her forties knows better than that.

What could I have said? How could I have proved my ovary was healthy or that my appendix didn't need to be removed? What could I, a woman without medical expertise, have accused a respected oncologist of with no evidence? How could I have claimed my body as mine while lying unconscious in the operating room? How could my hunch that the doctor had performed unnecessary procedures for his personal gain possibly have any weight in court? Did I now, just as I did twenty years ago, sanction the surgeon's behavior with my silence? Will my inaction be translated into: go ahead, do it to other women, count on my complicity. Enjoy your tee times, handsome.

I swallow hard, check the local time in Hong Kong. It's 9:00 p.m. Not too early for a G&T. I fix myself one with more T than G and allow myself to say it one last time. My ovary.

There.

I said it.

I'm done mourning.

Water under the bridge.

12

Writers of Color

I learned English as an adult. I speak it with a heavy Colombian accent, which I love—it makes my speech unique—with the same intensity I hate—it makes my speech unintelligible to some. Not often, but often enough to make me self-conscious. Every time I prepare for a reading of my own work, I find sentences that require too many silent vowels and diphthongs. I keep running into enunciations that remain a mystery to me—the price one pays for learning a foreign language late in life. If given the option, I would never read my work in front of an audience. The thing is, when I write, I do not have to know the forty-four sounds of English—twenty-five consonant sounds and nineteen vowel sounds—five short vowels, six long vowels, three diphthongs, two "oo" sounds, and three r-controlled vowel sounds. When I write, my keyboard does not notice my accent, does not tilt its head to one side and ask, Please say that again. When I write, my world is soundless; my fingers, the keyboard, the screen, and I communicate in a nonverbal language of keystrokes and clicks. When I write, I don't have an accent.

Maybe because I don't like being the only writer I know who reads her work in English with a foreign lilt, I continuously look for other Latinx writers with an accent. I'm sure there are many out there with enunciations thick as mud. I just don't know any. I need a community of twisted tongues, harsh digraphs, and creative ways to land a sentence containing a Future Perfect Continuous tense.

I find the answer to my prayers in a literary journal: a writing workshop for writers of color. I sign up for the travel writing workshop, and a few weeks later, I embark on my twenty-hour-plus (I am temporarily living in the Middle East) journey to my newly found family of heavy-tongued fellow writers. A clan of my own actually exists.

After the transatlantic flight, I'm jetlagged and exhausted. I sit on a bench outside the airport, waiting for a taxi. A woman sits next to me. She is white, with blue veins showing through the paper-thin skin of her arms and legs. She makes small talk, and I don't hide my disinterest, but she gets my attention when she says that she is there to attend a writing workshop for writers of color. I turn my brown face forty-five degrees and stare silently into her white, blue-eyed face.

"Oh, I'm 8 percent Cherokee," she says, after a few awkward silent seconds.

I am confused. I don't understand how a white American woman could attend a workshop for writers of color, like me, based on her 8 percent Cherokee ancestry. Would I, a dark-skinned woman, be accepted into a workshop for white writers? I wonder.

When I arrive at the conference site, the first thing that catches my eye is the number of white people. I'm an introvert. I don't make friends easily. I'm the one walking around at a party, drink in hand, mortified by the prospect of being approached. So, I do what I do best. I walk around, ears pricked, antenna out, radar on. I don't hear foreign accents. In fact, I think I'm the only writer attending this conference who doesn't speak unaccented American English. There are skin tones in many hues of dark, don't get me wrong. I see everything from almost black to deep dark brown to slightly tanned. It's all there. The sight of dark-skinned writers excites me; the sound of their voices doesn't. If I were blind and asked to find a name for the gathering, I'd go for Workshop for American Writers.

I soon learn that most white writers I encounter have, or claim to have, non-white ancestors. I have no way to prove or disprove their claims. A few have Native American blood; others have Mexican heritage. One woman tells me that her great-great, some ancestor from way back, was Irish. Irish. A couple of writers have African blood (Yoruba from Nigeria), some others are first-generation Indians. But nobody has an accent. I'm convinced they will immediately disregard my prose if they hear my accent. I retreat into my self-conscious shell, feeling like an oddity.

Who am I? According to my DNA analysis, my ancestry can be broken down into three main categories: 44 percent European, 37 percent East Asian and Native American, and 13 percent Sub-Saharan African. Does this mean that I, a Colombian woman, can file as Native American or as Black in the USA? If the writer I met in the workshop could claim to be "of color" because of her 8 percent Cherokee, could I register myself as white with 37 percent European ancestry? Who decides this type of thing?

The workshop leader is a woman hard not to love. She is a laid-back half-Norwegian, half-Nigerian ex-Buddhist nun and travel writer who laughs often and is genuinely interested in our efforts to be better at this travel writing thing. She doesn't have a foreign accent. In my group, there are two Indians—two of the most intelligent, eloquent people I've ever met in my life; one is a university professor, the other a physician. They don't speak English with a foreign accent. A Korean woman with an infectious laugh speaks perfect Californian English, a Ghanaian with skin dark as a moonless night, a killer smile, and hips like a shrine. She doesn't have a Ghanaian accent. The soft-spoken young Chicana of Filipino descent has impish dimples and consistently writes about ancestral rituals. Her English is unaccented. I sit quietly at one end of the table, take all this Americanness in, and feel like an outsider. I misled myself when I mistook color for accent. Everyone around me speaks English like they own it.

My dream of having a clan of borrowers of the English language won't come true here.

There is a reading downtown which I've been looking forward to attending. It is hosted by a travel magazine that has sent me encouraging personalized rejection letters a couple of times. The organizer is a renowned writer in the travel writing circle, and he has invited our group to the reading. The bigwigs of the travel writing scene will be there. I can't wait to shake hands with the editor who has rejected my work but encouraged me to submit more.

The day before the reading, our group leader shares the news with us about the event: there will be mostly white people at the event. I hope she is joking because, as far as I'm concerned, the audience could be green, and I'd still want to go, but the stern faces I see around the table and the Well, No Way, I Don't Think So comments I hear tells me that my fellow writers find the color of the audience off-putting. I don't understand the root of their discomfort or what the audience's skin color has to do with writing. When the question Who still wants to go? is asked, I'm the only one with a raised hand.

We end up going. By the time we arrive, the hip library located in a swanky hotel is packed. I buy a glass of overpriced wine and happily sit in the back, ready to be taken to faraway places with each story. Some of my fellow writers are sulking, compulsively looking at the clock, rolling their eyes, acting like children forced to go on an unwanted field trip. A couple of them bitterly complain about the prices of the wine and take exception that there is wine at all—the presence of alcohol gives the event a bourgeois air that doesn't settle well with them.

The reading is going well. Nothing breathtaking so far, but a few lighthearted travel stories. We clap at the end of one reading, and the next reader goes to the podium. The writer who had vehemently opposed coming to an event full of white people and who earlier had complained about the price of wine, interjects as soon as the reader grabs the microphone.

"Hell, no. What the fuck?"

Suddenly, she gets up and heads to the door.

"I am not here to listen to no Barbie."

I look up and realize that the new reader is tall, white, has long legs, and a blond mane that cascades down to her lower back. The disgruntled fellow writer leaves the room before the woman with long legs starts reading; a couple of writers follow her.

When the reading ends, we go out looking for a bite and a drink. There is a beautiful place across the street from the venue. It's dimly lit, has a massive fireplace and low leather bean bags. We walk in and immediately walk out. It's too bourgeois, someone in the group decides. We go somewhere else, but some of the writers decide that this place is also too posh; we are writers, for god's sake, not high-class snobs. We need to go somewhere else. And somewhere else we go, but that other place is too chic, too fancy, so we go somewhere else and that somewhere else is also too upper class. We go somewhere else. Before I know it, we are taking the Metro, or the subway, or a couple of taxis, or public transport, I don't remember, until we end up in some hole-in-the-wall. It is a Korean diner serving delicious food, and I wonder why these writers consider themselves too street to eat at a nice-looking, well-located place. Conversely, why do they consider certain places not worthy of our presence? What's so special about us, a group of word lovers looking for a bite? But more importantly, I think while I savor my kimchi, what would have happened if a couple of white people attending the reading had walked out because a non-white writer took the microphone?

A few days later, we go to a bar a short walk away. We arrive just before happy hour, and the place is empty. It's just us, a whole bunch of writers having a beer. A faculty member, a renowned Black poet I've never heard of, sports a T-shirt with names written on it. I don't know who they are. Too many of them to be a musical band, I think. But the names mean something to everyone who comes to admire her shirt, and I wonder what's wrong with me. Why do I not know what they know? I consciously decided to stop watching the news a few years ago, and I have since lived in happy oblivion. Coming across as stupid, unaware, or indifferent, I realize now, is the unforeseeable price I pay for this personal decision of living in isolation. A few patrons arrive. They are young, white, don office attire, leather briefcases, and some women are in expensive-looking high heels. They are the epitome of corporate success. Their presence stirs something among the writers that I can't name. It's a public space after all, not a Writers of Color Only bar. The Black poet with the T-shirt goes around our tables and shares her plan: every fifteen minutes, we, writers of color, stand up and shout a name from her T-shirt. I decide not to partake. I don't understand what we are doing or why we are doing it.

Emmet Till! The writers shout.

I sit at the bar and observe. Two more writers, who also decide not to participate, join in and start small talk about our personal lives. Married, single, divorced, with a partner, without a partner, in love, heartbroken, children, no children. One of them asks me where my husband is from, and I say Scotland.

"Oh, not Colombian?" she asks.

I smile nervously. I feel like I'm being quizzed.

"No, he is Scottish."

The writers give each other funny looks.

"What?" I ask.

"Is he a Black Scotsman?" they want to know.

I see where this is going.

"No, he is a white, blue-eyed, true-blue Scot from the High-lands."

I have failed the test. Their faces tell me so.

"Why didn't you marry a brother?"

"Why would I marry a brother?" I want to crack a silly joke about hillbillies. I don't. "I have always been attracted to white men."

They make no attempt to disguise their disgust. They are disappointed in me, a brown Colombian who likes white skin.

Trayvon Martin!! The writers shout, much to the surprise of the white patrons, who smile dumb, polite, but inquisitive smiles, and ask what's going on. The writers of color are mum. It is our secret. Their secret. I still don't know what they are doing.

"I don't understand," the writer to my right says, "why you, a POC, would not marry another POC?"

My heart races. I don't know what POC is. I think the People of China but discard it immediately. Point of Contact doesn't fit the occasion either. Pirates of the Caribbean is entirely out of context.

I shrug my shoulders. "What do you mean?"

More yuppies arrive. They seem to like what they see: a large group of adults with skin color darker than theirs. They are congenial and express interest in knowing what the shouting is about because they also want to shout. Nobody talks to them or smiles back when they grin their white-collar, slightly tipsy smiles.

Whenever all the different groups—poetry, travel, fiction, etc.— get together, the air feels heavy with discontent. I came here looking for a community of like-accented writers, and what I've gotten so far is a community of writers with a lot to say, their hearts laden with centuries-old grievances. I take that back; discontent is not the right word; it's too simplistic. Imagine what happens when people who, through systemic failure, have consistently been denied their place in society get the chance to speak out. Every word comes with a bang and a boom.

We gather in the conference room on the day we are supposed to hold group readings—fiction, travel, memoir, etc. The temperature rises with each passage read; words become lethal weapons, poems are hurled into the air like Molotov cocktails, and slowly a sort of mini-revolution starts to brew. There are rants about cultural imperialism, essays on neocolonialism, references to Uncle Tom (note to self: read *Uncle Tom's Cabin*), denunciations of post-colonial language, and systemic oppression. Someone reads a poem about breaking chains. Before I know it, everyone is chanting revolution, fists up in the air, revolution, clenched hands pumping, revolution, head bobbing, revolution, feet stomping, goddammed revolution. The last time I fist pumped and chanted revolution, I was a fourteen-year-old communist-wannabe convinced I could fix my screwed-up country by shouting slogans and singing "The Internationale" anthem: Stand up all victims of oppression / For the tyrants fear your might . . . It's a moment of unity, and as such, it is sacred, like a congregation caught up in a moment of rapture, like that instant at a music concert where everyone around you is as high on tempo and life as you are and the whole place feels like a shrine. Yet, I can't bring myself to join in. It feels false and childish. Like I'm fourteen again and going out of my way just to fit in with my comrades.

The political undertone of the gathering takes me by surprise. Right now, I want to write about place, to learn from my ex-Buddhist nun how to describe landscapes more evocatively, to make the readers feel, taste, and hear places they have never been to. Right now, I'm too naive or too blind or too removed from the American reality to politicize traveling. It would be years after this event, after I showed my daughter a draft of this essay— the harshest first reader a writer could ask for—that she made me realize that traveling and travel writing are highly political, especially for a woman of color like me. My daughter wrote: *I understand that you expected the travel workshop not to be political. However, every part of our life is politicized—especially a travel workshop for writers of color. Politics dictate what you can do or say, what options you have for every aspect of your life. The personal is political. Pretending that life isn't political is for people who have no stake in it, and that's not you.*

Ouch, and yes, Paula, thank you. I needed your shoulder-shaking words to see the whole picture, to realize the obvious: I, a dark-skinned Colombian, get, in general, a different treatment than my white husband does when we travel together. In some countries, white skin is associated with wealth; dark skin is not. My husband screams purchasing power as we walk hand in hand into a Thai shop, a Cambodian restaurant, a Nepalese hotel, a Moroccan seaport; I don't. Often, we get asked at check-in counters if we are traveling together; I believe this question is asked because anti-miscegenation views are still ingrained in people's psyches. Once, while visiting my husband, who was working in Turkmenistan, a security guard stopped us in the lobby of his hotel: Sorry, sir, no prostitutes allowed here. Humiliation and misunderstanding aside, it was true. The five-star hotel did not allow its guests—mostly American and British—to bring sex workers in unless they were high-end Russian call girls who could pass as their wives without tarnishing the hotel's reputation.

I have lived in two Middle Eastern countries for a total of fourteen years. I am used to being ignored at restaurants when the waiters come to our table to ask, "How's your food, sir?" and I am entirely bypassed. In the Middle East, I become a pocket of air in my husband's company, not for being dark but for being a woman. I live at the crossroads of religion, culture, history, and politics. I have learned that my husband is much more successful at making things happen in the bank, getting answers at the immigration department, sorting out visas, paying bills, getting a plumber. How could I ignore how political travel is for a woman of color?

I suffer from chronic wanderlust. I am an avid reader, a traveler, and a cultural anthropologist. At the intersection of the three, I have come across many travel narratives where the writers describe their experiences with the "Noble Savages" they encountered or present themselves as the saviors of a group of people (usually dark) who would have perished without their intervention, or cross oceans and mountains on so-called spiritual journeys only to "find themselves" in faraway lands peopled by the oh-so-exotic other.

Pretending that life isn't political is for people who have no stake in it, and that's not you.

Ouch, and yes, Paula. Thank you.

On the last day of the workshop, we meet outside the campus at a big auditorium. There is a faculty reading, and everyone is abuzz with curiosity about what our teachers will read. Then they take the microphone one by one and let us see why they were chosen to lead the workshops. Toward the end, a Black poet takes the stage. She is known for incendiary slam poetry. Her poem starts as something mundane. She is at a McDonald's having a bite when a white woman asks if she can sit with her as no tables are available. And that was it. The poem progresses into a rant about the white woman ignoring the poet's No and sitting at the table anyway, forcing her to share a space she claimed as hers earlier. What started as a simple exchange at a McDonald's flourishes into an explosive denunciation. I understand that someone imposing herself at my table after I have refused is inconsiderate, to say the least. I also believe in sisterhood and therefore assume that if there are no tables available and another woman asks me to share mine, it is only civil to allow her to sit with me, regardless of her skin color. But quickly realize I'm missing her point, for this poem is not about not wanting to share space. This poem is about a white person invading a Black person's space. The table represents the Black woman's world, culture, and history. It is a hermit crab poem, something she created from the shell of another, like the hermit crab that lives its life within the shell of another mollusk. The poem is not about what happened in the restaurant for McDonald's is just the shell she used to slam the system. From the french fries, the poem morphs into a denunciation of the master-slave culture that brought the first Black people to the New World. The poet becomes livelier and livelier with each passing minute; each stanza a reignited torch, each calculated pause laden with contained anger. The poet is a flame thrower; it seems as though if she doesn't release all that energy, she will self-combust. So she releases her poetic atomic bomb. She sets the auditorium ablaze. There is ardent fist-pumping, chaotic feet stomping, and interjections: damn right, you tell them, word, no more, no more!

I leave the auditorium feeling keenly alive, feeling Berkeley pulsating under my skin with every step I take on my way back to my hotel room. I turn on my laptop and read most of the night.

The things I learned and ruminated:

POC: A person of color. How could I be a POC and not know it? I don't want to be known as a POC or a writer of color. My skin color doesn't define, confine, or propel my writing. My experience of the world transcends the edges of my skin. I want to be read as if my written words were diamonds: transparent and colorless. I don't want my work to be referred to as the work of a writer of color. I don't write with my skin. I don't write in hues of brown, light chocolate, dark café au lait, or caramel. I write with my heart and my brain, both of which, I presume, are of the same universal color as the rest.

I don't want to be called a heterosexual writer. I don't write with my sexual preference. What I do behind doors has nothing to do with what I write. Or at least I hope it doesn't.

I don't want to be known as a Buddhist writer because I practice Buddhism. And so on and so forth. I want to be referred to as a woman who can write.

A paradigm that begs the question: Is that how it feels to be white and married to a non-white? Never did I imagine being chastised for being married to a white man. Why would that matter? What kind of allegiance does my skin pledge to in matters of the heart?

Some people who appear white to me don't consider themselves so, a realization that boggles my mind. A writer friend of mine, whose skin color I would confidently describe as white—for lack of a better qualifier—calls herself brown because she is Puerto Rican. How could I find this so confusing just now in my forties? Would you not be confused if I told you that I'm white after seeing me—a brown woman? Surely all these paths are two-way streets.

Trayvon Martin: I have seen your picture many times. I recognize your piercing eyes and the white hoodie. You were shot by an overzealous citizen who killed you under the protection granted by Florida's Stand Your Ground law.

Dontre Hamilton, you were shot just a few months before the writing workshop. Your schizophrenia and erratic behavior were the excuses your killer used to put fourteen bullets into your body.

Other black men will be shot dead before the end of the year.

Ezel Ford, a twenty-five-year-old with the mental capacity of an eight-year-old, will be pinned to the ground and shot three times in the back.

Tamir Rice, you will not get to celebrate your thirteenth birthday. Your killer will not think twice before shooting you dead—your crime: carrying a replica toy Airsoft gun.

Eric Garner, you will not celebrate Christmas. You are about to die when a police officer puts you in a chokehold.

John Crawford III, soon you will be walking into a Wal-Mart holding a BB gun. This will cost you your life.

Michael Brown, your Don't Shoot cry won't stop your killer from firing twelve bullets in your direction, six of which will hit your Black body, all from the front.

Laquan McDonald, there will be something off about your gait. The way you walk will be perceived as so erratic, so terrifying, so threatening that your killer will shoot you dead as you walk away from him.

Antonio Martin, you live two miles from Michael Brown, and like him, you will not wake up on Christmas Day.

Jerame Reid, you will not see the new year. One day before this year is over; you will be shot in the chest as you are exiting your car, unarmed, your hands at chest level.

White people will be shot, too, as well as brown. For them, there will be no organized protests or T-shirts memorializing their names. If we were to memorialize all those shot unjustly by a system quick to draw its weapons and shoot anything perceived as a threat, we would need whole quilts sewn to one another. The thread the color of blood, the batting corrosive and congealed, the edges heavy with street grit, mouths wide open against the concrete, teeth shattering on the curb; the top fabric a tangled mess of hands up shaking with fear and contained anger, the backing material a chorus of Don't Shoot, Don't You Fucking Shoot.

It has been seven weeks since I began to observe the rules of social distancing imposed by our current situation. I have time to look up the poet known for incendiary slam poetry. I have binge-watched her videos on YouTube, some of which made me weep in solidarity, not because of our skin color—two different shades of brown—but because we are women. She talks about her body in such a way that I feel in my bones all the damage that has been done to hers. I look up the Black poet with the t-shirt and see all her credentials and accolades. I read her poetry, and although I don't read poetry in English, I am ashamed of not knowing her work until now. I revisit the names of those Black boys and men printed on her t-shirt, those human beings whose unnecessarily violent deaths galvanized society, birthed the Black Lives Matter movement, and denounced systemic brutality. Where have I been all my life?

I write about the writers' workshop without suspicion, without anger, without judgment. I write about what I found in them and within me. I learned that being white is almost as complicated as being black or brown. What makes a person white? Their skin color—like my Puerto Rican friend who appears very white to me but considers herself brown—or their provenance? I have a white friend who was born and raised in Zimbabwe when it was called Rhodesia. He later came to the USA, fell in love with and married a white American woman, and became an American citizen. When the census guy knocked at their door, my friend demanded to be recorded as African American, which he is, for all intents and purposes. The census guy refused. He thought it was a joke. How could a white man be African American?

A few years ago, while living in Florida, a sort of news exhaustion came over me. News was a misnomer for unsurprising information that failed to contribute to my awareness of the world.

I started to call them Olds rather than News, stopped buying newspapers, turned the television off, and gradually retreated into a bubble of quiet ignorance. For years, I have found snippets of the world through my timid activity on social media enough to make me recoil back into my deaf-to-the-world office. But it's the year 2020, and my daughter has read the draft of this essay and has popped my bubble of oblivion with the sharp tip of her pen: *The privilege of deciding not to know what goes on in the world is an immense luxury that American POC can't afford.*

Ouch, and yes, Paula. Thank you. Turning a blind eye to the current situation and choosing ignorance over knowledge is an obscene luxury, a sin I can no longer commit. People of all colors are marching, protesting diligently, and painstakingly working to change the status quo—to tip the scale so that we all stand the same chance of living fulfilling lives. I see their names, their faces, and their tragic ends. I see them gasping for air, uttering their last words, and drawing their last breaths. One called out for his mother. One was killed in her sleep. One was maced to death.

I can't breathe.

I can't breathe.

I can't breathe.

I can't breathe.

I can't breathe.

I can't breathe.

I can't breathe.

I can't breathe.

I can't breathe.

I can't breathe.

I can't breathe.

Eleven times.

I am still suspicious of the news broadcasters telling me what's going on in the world, because they have power and that power comes with an agenda. I'm terrified of misinformation, of being misled, manipulated, and seduced by the appeal of believing what everybody believes, that dangerously comforting "common knowledge" hastily drawn from headlines and individual imagination. I'm afraid of the people who refuse to admit that we have a problem, who fix "this mess" over drinks or coffee with flippant rhetoric that lacks any knowledge of history, and who think that compassion is an overrated word used by hippies, feminists, and do-gooders. We have a problem that can only be fixed if we stop thinking according to our skin color or sexuality. Black Lives Matter is not just for Black people; non-Black people need such a movement more than anybody else. Feminism is not just for women; it is for everyone who agrees that men and women have the same rights under the law. LGBTQIA is the school that all heterosexuals should attend to learn about respect, how to be an ally, and to understand that behind the Love is Love slogan is the core of our existence.

I read the news.

George Floyd.

Breonna Taylor.

Zohra, an eight-year-old girl illegally employed as a maid, was tortured and killed by her employers in Rawalpindi, Pakistan, for letting their pet parrots escape. Read again—an eight-year-old girl working as a maid. Think modern slavery. Shiver. Feel ashamed of being human.

Atatiana Jefferson.

Dreasjon "Sean" Reed.

Seven soldiers raped a thirteen-year-old Emberá Indigenous girl in Colombia. Seven grown-up men trained to serve and protect took turns breaking a little girl half their weight. What kind of men are we raising?

Aura Rosser.

Ahmaud Arbery.

Imagine every single Santa Monica, California, inhabitant living in a cage. Outrageous, right? Unfathomable. Crazy. Yet, that's about the amount of undocumented immigrant children living in cages at detention centers all over the USA.

A noose. A door pull rope left in the garage of Bubba Wallace, the only Black NASCAR race car driver, was initially thought to be a noose. That a knot becomes a noose is a sign of our tragic times.

Sean Monterrosa.

Jamel Floyd.

Lynchings. In recent weeks at least five men—four Black and one Latinx—have been found hanging in public across the US. These deaths are being investigated and could have been suicides, but the mere fact that they could be lynchings makes me want to crawl under my bed, go to sleep, and unread and unsee. Scratch that. Reading and watching the news make me want to scream, cry, and rage; the news makes me want to put fists through walls, vomit, and switch species.

Yes, we have a problem, not just as a nation but as a race.

It's been a few years since the workshop for writers of color. I now understand things that I didn't back then. For example, I know now that the best way to understand collective anger, whether openly expressed or bottled up, is as seen within a historical or sociopolitical context. Those choosing to stand outside a collective expression of anger are responsible for educating themselves on the matter; those who learn history from movies and news headlines should shy away from the belief that a handful of mis-led looters speak for generations of slave descendants. I understand that the names imprinted on the writer's T-shirt are an incomplete memorial, for there are not enough T-shirts in the world to stamp the names of those executed, tased, raped, tortured, and maimed with the complicity of the system that was designed to protect them. I understand that when a white woman invades a Black woman's space at a McDonald's when this Black woman has fought all her life to claim her spot in the world, the act is much more than a microaggression; it no longer is one more stripe on the zebra; it is the insult that broke the proverbial camel's back, it's a "Really, white woman? I said no. This table is all the space I'm allowed today, and I'm claiming it as mine and mine alone. I will not share this, this, this, this, with you."

I get it now. Not all of it, but I'm closer.

I've been perusing the workshop website. Faculty, board, and alumni are hugely successful, collectively, and individually. I don't know if its mission statement has changed or if I didn't read it when I applied. It is clearly stated. The workshop is ". . . the only multi-genre workshop for writers of color in the US founded by and for writers of color as a revolution." A revolution. How did I miss this? It continues. "At the intersection of social justice and artistic mastery, it builds individual mastery and artistic communities that create new cultural understandings, changing how individuals and societies perceive themselves." An intersection of social justice and art, which is precisely what I do. I work with marginalized women, gather their stories, and voice them on paper. We do the same. The only difference is that they don't have an accent when delivering their stories to a live audience. And in light of what they do and have accomplished, my wish for a family of men and women who write with the fluidity of water and speak with r's heavy like lead seems petty and juvenile.

Who am I? I know this much, I am a Colombian woman, mother, sister, wife, writer, teacher, activist, and women's rights advocate. I learned English late in life and speak it with a heavy accent. I'm in my fifties now, and I have to admit, I wish I could go back to the workshop for writers of color knowing what I know now. I wish I had written this essay earlier so that Paula could have read it earlier also, and opened my eyes to the reality that she lives day in and day out in the USA and from which I am so far removed.

Who is she? She is a woman of color with fire in her belly. She is a psychologist, Navy veteran, wife, daughter, and a terrific first reader, this much I know. When I brought her to the USA, my command of the English language was basic, and hers was nonexistent at five years of age. But she picked it up, as children do, mastered it, made it her mother tongue, and speaks it fluently, beautifully, eloquently. The country she inhabits in 2020 is different from the country I brought her to in 1992. We are not the same people either. We arrived in the USA, voiceless and powerless. Two Colombian girls who had never seen snow learned to navigate this utterly foreign culture blindly, clumsily. Now we are American citizens, no longer powerless and not voiceless. I hope Paula gets out of bed every day and uses her power and voice to get involved, fight injustice wherever she sees it, and vote for people who can carry her strength to Washington. I hope she partakes in this revolution, fist-pumping and all. I hope she can enjoy a good story because it is well told and not because of the skin color of its reader. I hope she carries a torch to illuminate the path for those who can't see the way ahead. I hope she has learned that there are many ways to push and shove and does it unabashedly as she sees fit. I hope she continues being kind, soft, sympathetic, and aware of the world. I hope she doesn't forget where she came from: a long line of poor, borderline-illiterate women who shielded themselves from gender inequality armed with nothing but faith and strength, a long line of women who moved mountains for generations so that she and I could be where and who we are today: two immigrant women fighting a good fight, she in perfect English, her mama in a heavily accented one.

13

Love on the Iditarod Trail

I come from a long line of good Catholic wives. Both my grand-mothers remained married to the same men until death did them part. My mother married my father when she was nine-teen and kept her vows even after he abandoned her with six children. She refused to remove her wedding ring and remained devoted to the memory of their brief life together throughout his silent twenty years of desertion. My sisters also are good, faithful wives. They have built solid families that have known only one father. My brother's wife is also an exemplary spouse. He got her pregnant when she was sixteen; they are still going strong fifty years later. The women in my family don't take un-necessary risks and are neither reckless nor mercurial about their career paths. They retired from the same professions they chose in their teens and have never lived outside Colombia. They are austere. Solid. Reliable. Unmovable.

I'm not like them.

I met him at a conference in Houston, the halfway point be-tween his home in Alaska and mine in Medellín, a fact that I interpreted as a good omen. It started with inquisitive looks we exchanged across the conference room during talks and work-shops. Soon, we were sitting next to each other, having lunch together, and dragging our feet at the end of the day, always looking for excuses to stay behind and talk. Things unfolded quickly. I found his company comforting. He possessed a peace-ful aura and seemed to walk under an umbrella of lightness and transparency, precious qualities I had never seen in a man. By the end of the week, I found myself craving his quiet company, and the thought of returning to the crushing weight of the complexities of my life in Colombia was unbearable. After the conference, he asked me to go with him to Galveston. He wanted to show me the damage hurricane Andrew had caused a few years back. As I remember, we were walking down the deserted beach when I spotted something wriggling in the sand. It's a shrimp, he said. I had seen shrimp only in supermarkets. They were pink and soft, frozen things ready to be eaten; they didn't resemble this dark crescent inside a shell waving its antennae and whiskers wildly in the sand. I held it in my hand and started to run to the sea to give the shrimp a chance, to send it back home, but he stopped me. Leave it, he said. Dropping it back into the ocean will only prolong its agony. His cruelty took me by surprise. How could a man who looked so gentle be so cold? Leave it, he repeated, taking the thing from my hand and flung it into the air. It's already dead.

But he had kind blue eyes, gentle hands, and an easy smile, so I said yes when he asked me to leave it all behind a few months later and move in with him in Anchorage.

He had been precisely the unlikely and correct combination of person for me—stoic, calm, and collected, the perfect tether for my kite-like nature, yet equally intellectual and rugged, one weekend in the mountains hunting, hiking, fishing, followed by a week of office work as a geologist. For these reasons, it hadn't seemed reckless to have married him two months after quitting my job as a petroleum engineer in Colombia and arriving in Alaska. On the contrary, it appeared that not marrying him would have been a reckless decision. He married me because he loved me; I married him because I liked to be loved by him and wanted to love him back, because he was the best man who had ever walked into my life, and because I'm an intelligent woman and smart women marry good men.

However, soon after the honeymoon, our two cultures came into such opposition that we might as well have lived in different countries. Both of us were engineers, but intellectually we inhabited different realms. Mine was filled with poetry, music, politics, and foreign movies; his with fishing holes, hunting rifles, wildlife, and trees. Domestically, he preferred heavy furniture, hugging La-Z-Boy recliners by the fireplace and dining tables of weighty solid wood. He liked predictability, certainty, things that didn't move. He liked things that came into his life to stay for good. He lived a life of soft, precise, and clean contours. My taste had emptied his living room, replaced his bulky furniture with two sleek rocking chairs by the window, given away his dated sun-blocking blinds, and exchanged the carpet and the bear pelts on the floor for wooden parquet that befitted my love for dancing. His country music CDs were now stacked behind rows of world music. The air in the house was filled with Brazilian sambas, Dominican merengues, Puerto Rican salsa, Phillip Glass' strident violins, Hakka songs, and pygmy chants. I came into his life like a derailed steam train, and he, in his quiet way, rather than finding my over-the-top passion off-putting, had fearlessly turned toward it, attracted by the heat I threw off.

Then, one day, during the annual Iditarod race, I felt light and malleable. I let my guard down and decided to immerse myself in his world, dive into his beloved outdoors, and see if I could fall in love with Alaska. I put on my thermals and my snow boots, my mittens and my gloves, my snowsuit and my fur hat. I got on the back of our snow machine and let my husband drive us to the Iditarod trail to witness a section of the Last Great Race on Earth: a sled dog race covering over one thousand miles from

Anchorage, in south-central Alaska where we lived, to Nome on the western Bering Sea coast.

In Wasilla, we met his brothers' convoy of snow machines. They dressed in camouflage outfits, full-face helmets that had seen better times, and scratched amber goggles. One of them had his cheek swollen with chewing tobacco, and a hole in his jacket had been covered with duct tape. At some point, my husband stopped, lifted the visor of his helmet to rearrange his balaclava, and either the wind or the cold did something to his eyes. It turned them a much brighter shade of blue than I remembered ever seeing, which made me wonder if I had ever really seen his eyes, as I encircled my arms around his waist. The cold had given him chapped lips and a pink nose. I also lifted my visor. Snowflakes fell fat and playful on my tongue. He looked at me in the rearview mirror and smiled as if saying *attagirl*. Before he turned the ignition again, he laughed out loud at his brothers throttling their machines behind us. *Rednecks*, he called them. They wore green hunting gear even though they were not chasing game, only the distant bark of the huskies running the race. His brothers' children howled like beasts, steam billowed out of their gaping mouths. We howled back, and together we formed a pack of lousy wolves. His father rode pillion on one of the snow machines. During the ride, the old man turned his head in our direction and gave us a variety of cheerful signals with his gloved hand, the other firmly fastened around his son's waist: a military salute, a peace sign, a vigorous wave. Everyone was high on Iditarod. On a bend, my in-laws revved their machines and sped up, leaving behind a cloud of powdery snow that looked like sand. For a few seconds, we were blinded. When we emerged from the cloud, my husband swerved the snow machine to avoid hitting a tree. Until that day, I hadn't known he was that strong. That agile. That swift. He pointed at a bald eagle's nest perched up in a tree. How could he possibly maneuver the machine, keep an eye on the blinding white path we were making, and still look around for life? He turned his head forty-five degrees. *It's beautiful*, he shouted. *It is*, I shouted back, even though I hadn't seen the nest, only the impossibly blue skies and the vast winter wilderness of western Alaska.

We made our way to Knik, Yentna Station, Skwentna, all the way to Finger Lake to meet the mushers: the drivers of the dog sleds. At this point, we were 123 miles from Anchorage. Home seemed out of reach—a liberating thought.

I took pictures of the dogs, beautiful furry, blue-eyed creatures who all appeared identical to me. *No*, he said. *There are different breeds*. He pointed at the Alaskan Malamutes, Japanese Akitas, Siberian and Alaskan huskies, the Eurohounds, and the German Shorthaired Pointers. There were Samoyeds, Chinooks, and a whole pile of crossbreeds. How could a man know so much about dogs and so little about Pablo Neruda's poetry, the revolutions fought down the border with Mexico, the nuances of the Spanish language, magical realism, or the tragedy of Los Desaparecidos?

His brothers decided to follow the mushers farther up the trail. After everyone had left the colossal bonfire at Finger Lake, he recited the names of upcoming checkpoints like a childhood prayer: Rainy Pass, Rohn, Nikolai, McGrath, Takotna, and Ophir. As we got back on the snow machine, ready to head back to Anchorage, he told me the names of the towns up north, gorgeous Inuit fairytale-sounding names such as Unalakleet, Shaktoolik, Koyuk, and others that led to Nome. He drove slowly, looking for wildlife left, right, and above.

When he pulled over, the sun had started to come down methodically, as if every inch of its plunge into the horizon had a specific purpose. As I remember, this was the quietest and the whitest bend north of the Tropic of Cancer. The air smelled of nothing, like crushed diamonds, like infinity. We removed our helmets and the neoprene balaclavas, dismounted the machine, and stood there in front of each other, examining eyes, noses, mouths, foreheads, suddenly, so many destinations.

There were no huskies, no mushers, no iron dogs in sight. It felt like we were the last people left on earth. There were no epiphanies. No magic. No words. We made no promises, denied nothing, didn't offer anything. We kissed hungrily and let our snow bibs collapse into shabby circles around our ankles. We fell into each other's arms like we were near death, and the old ritual possessed us. In this constellation of body parts, I inhaled him, guided him in with cold-numb fingers, and swallowed him like a sinkhole. I became keenly, expansively aware of the life around us. Ptarmigans and eagles did their dance over our heads. I visualized my heart raucously thudding against his chest—my breasts pressing against the knobs of his ribs—so close to the bone, like his own heart, and I wondered if we'd be able after a while to tell the two apart. I thought: This is the kind of moment that can change the world. Big words and the amorphous ideas they represent became simple and clear under his touch. A word like "evil" became "sandstorm" instead. And just like that, life regained its plasticity. We could say the Lord's Prayer and change it into "and lead us not into temptation, but deliver us from sandstorms, amen." A new kind of love descended upon me. It filled the arctic wind with a presence unmistakably larger than anything I had experienced before, a tangible certainty that surpassed longing, a type of love that, in its finitude, felt different from human love. And I knew, in my heart of hearts, that I would never love anything or anyone with the same savage finality.

I'm sure every time our tongues collided, a great gray owl blinked its yellow eyes, and the aurora borealis brewed in a corner of the sky. He held my face in his cold hands and looked at me, through me, past me. There we were, his flesh against my flesh, our bones moving together like synchronized swimmers. With him inside me, I imagined a parallel life together. In that instant, I believed that maybe, just maybe, we could sort things out, unlock the mysteries of each other's hearts, disarm, let go, surrender, live.

It was a good life. We would be the family in the two-story house on Westwind Drive, have a cocker spaniel named Cinnamon, a hot tub in the backyard, and a motorhome in the driveway. We could have a child together who would look like him but think like me, which is to say, a little cherub with golden curls, milky skin, and deep blue eyes, who loved dancing, didn't believe in Santa, and made inappropriate jokes in Spanish-accented English. We would go to church, sing hymns in the car, say grace before our meals, and teach our child to fear God. We would have camping trips, the three of us and Cinnamon. We would pitch tents, start fires, and roast marshmallows on sticks. He would show me how to use a bow and arrow, and together we would skin caribou, hunt beautiful deer, and catch trout and king salmon in Mirror Lake. In this imagined life, I would learn how to stop our catch from flapping wildly in our canoe by delivering a blow to their heads. We would take our raft down chalky rivers, spot mountain goats from the road, pick blueberries in the prairie, and go ice skating on frozen lakes. We would make love twice a month, and I, lovingly and dutifully, would iron his underwear.

Snapshots of this beautiful yet unwanted life passed under my eyelids, and I saw our future selves in a flash. I would resemble my grandmother; my back bent like a sad bamboo shoot; he would look like his father with a face creased with age and regrets, like a worn map folded incorrectly one too many times.

This was precisely the life I dreaded living. This was not who I was or who I could ever be.

There came a final thrust, a muffled grunt, and a million stars exploded in the back of my head. A convoy of snow machines zoomed by, slapping snow onto our half-naked bodies, and just like that, the lovely moment was over. A wave of clarity washed over me. I understood then that I had been wrong in Galveston. I had wanted to put the shrimp in the water because I was after the cozy feeling of doing something right, even if it was wrong. On the other hand, he knew that my impulse was futile and cruel. The shrimp was already dead, but only he could see it.

We pulled our bibs up and dressed hurriedly, shivering with cold and recognition. The previous minutes of bliss had fixed nothing. We had emptied ourselves. We had nothing left to offer. We didn't possess the magic thread to keep the seams of our lives shut. He opened his mouth like he was about to speak. His chapped lips formed an O, then a silent line. There was something ominous in his eyes; they looked like a week of bad weather, as if this temporary afterlife of sex had cleared his mind and he could see me, not as the wife he would like me to be, but for who I really was: noisy, touchy-feely, foul-mouthed, a heavy smoker, and a red wine lover. A Latina with mutinous hair and unshaven legs known for her colorful repertoire of dirty jokes. A feminist, a Buddhist, a dancer. A pacifist who couldn't get along with his hunting friends. And I could tell that even after this realization, his blue eyes glimmered with something close to hope.

We'll be all right, he whispered in my ear. *Won't we?* I nodded, but our shared anxiety swelled and began to take space between us until it felt like the three of us would have to ride back to Anchorage. We kissed, and he hesitantly started the machine as if we were leaving something irretrievable behind. We rode in silence. Groggy with sated lust and doom. The cold air made its way through my winter clothing, pinning me to the back seat. I began to shiver. It wasn't only the below-freezing temperature that was making me cold. It was something the gravity of which seemed impossible to quantify. I was disappearing. Getting diluted into the vastness of his culture. My Colombian sense of justice, our collective fortitude in times of tragedy, our dark sense of humor in the face of natural and social disasters didn't translate easily into the Alaskan culture, where there are more airplanes per capita than anywhere else in the USA and probably the world; a culture where each year the state, through the Alaska Permanent Fund Dividend, pays every Alaskan resident (man, woman, and child) a cut of the revenue generated from a fund built with money from oil taxes. He came from a culture of natural abundance and capitalist comfort. I come from a country of struggle, political turmoil, and long stretches of bloodshed. The way we celebrate is also how we mourn, as if all of it were an inevitable part of being human.

It was dark when we exchanged our snow machine for the truck in Wasilla. Stretches of the Glenn highway had been recently sprayed with salt to melt the ice, and this, combined with the early image of Lot's wife, somehow made the idea of returning home unbearable. I thought of Susan and Deedee, the only female mushers competing that year in the Iditarod, headlamps on, battling howling gales, isolation, and hunger, tending to sick dogs, and dreaming of crossing the "burled arch," the official finish line in Nome. It dawned on me that marriage was more like the Iditarod race and less like the simple equation I had formulated in my head: smart woman + good-hearted man = forever happy. Maybe this was it, coupledom down the Iditarod trail of life with the reward being the comfort of believing you were doing what you were supposed to, without the fairytale butterflies and the glitter. Marriage as a slog, plodding on blindly, soldiering unflinchingly into the Nome of old age.

Forty-five minutes later, in the distance, I spotted Anchorage. My heart sank. I counted the number of its flickering lights—one, two, three, then ten, then more. I can do this, I told myself. I kept counting the lights until they were too close to be counted, and then I began again.

14

An Arab Man and an
English Woman Walk into a Bar

Qatar, October 2013. An English teacher and her French girl-friend walk into Sky View, a nightclub on a hotel's rooftop. They are dressed to impress. Their plan is simple: get a few fruity cocktails, dance to whatever the DJ has in store, smash that popular song with killer moves, turn a few heads, take pictures with Doha's skyline in the background, post them on Instagram and Facebook, make a few girly trips to the toilet to correct smeared mascara or reapply lipstick, take a taxi at the end of the night, sit in the back of the cab, and look at the pictures they just took at the club. Laugh. Slap each other in the arms. Stop it. It wasn't like that. No way. OMG. Delete that one. Get home, crash on the couch. Best night ever.

Maybe not. Maybe they plan to walk into the club, survey the patrons, make eye contact with the ones they like, let them pay for their drinks. Sure, a Cosmopolitan would be lovely. Thank you. Do I want to dance? Of course, I want to dance. A little twerking with a stranger has never hurt anyone. The night is young, they are young, and a river of Daiquiris, Piña Coladas, Negronis, Dry Martinis, and Moscow Mules runs wild that night. The young teachers bathe in it. A little smooch here and there. Not too much. Easy, cowboy. Keep your hands to yourself. Men are such pigs.

Same country, same night. An Arab man and his friend also walk into the club. They are locals and as such, they are not allowed to wear their national dress—long white tunics and headwear—where alcohol is served. The men walk in smelling of cologne, sporting expensive jeans, designer shirts, and trendy shoes. Their plan is simple: get a few beers, maybe a few whiskeys, dance to whatever the DJ has in store for the night, hit on a few women, see what happens, take pictures, post them on Instagram and Facebook, smoke a couple of cigars, drive home with the windows of their SUV rolled down, blast Arab music through their Bose speakers, steer the wheel with one hand, feel badass.

Maybe not. Maybe they plan to walk into the club, get hammered, hit on any pretty westerner—white women are so easy—and see what happens. Perhaps they plan to sit at the bar and stalk their prey. Wait until the pretty blond gets drunk and dry hump her on the dance floor. Maybe they plan to follow her to the bathroom and have her from behind as she bends over the toilet to vomit one too many martinis.

The Arab Man spots The English Teacher across the dance floor. They had met before. Once or twice. Maybe at someone's party or a BBQ in the desert. Yeah, they liked each other. The guy was cool—she remembers. The girl was hot—he remembers. They introduce their friends and they dance and drink with abandon. Tonight is a dreamt life finally come true. One a.m., last orders. C'mon, seriously? Booo, they want the party to go on forever. No problem, The Man says, the party is on chez moi. The girls look at each other. Why the hell not? They are tipsy and high on life. They get into his SUV, but soon the French girl changes her mind. She wants to go home. She is tired and ready for bed. The English Teacher is on fire. Fine, suit yourself. I'll party alone. They drop off the French teacher. They kiss goodbye. You okay? They ask each other in unison. Cool as a cucumber. I'll call you tomorrow. Bye. Partay!

I imagine the following day. A lonely falconer is out in the desert scouting for bird-training grounds. He is a Bedouin. A man hardened by life in the desert, with a face battered by cold winter winds and mean summer sandstorms; a man fluent in the language of birds of prey, thoroughly acquainted with a falcon's razor-sharp claws digging into his arm; a man who has seen it all and heard it all. One could say, an unimpressionable man. He spots smoke rising into the air a few yards before him, looks for evidence of a campsite, and finds none. He walks toward the billows of smoke, propelled by sheer curiosity but stops abruptly at the pit's edge. The unimpressionable man gasps, invokes Allah with broken utterances, grabs his head with both hands, then covers his nose as he peeks into the pit. Whatever is still burning smells like bad weather, like a rain of locusts, like the end of the world and everything precious in it. Whatever is still burning smells like heartbreak and tears. Like the phone call no mother ever wants to receive. Like the deafening silence that follows the unthinkable words: Are you such and such's mother? We are sorry to inform you that . . .

I imagine The English Teacher's Mother picking up the phone in England, trying to make sense of the words uttered over the phone. Someone is calling from the other side of the world to tell her about a body found in the desert. What's that have to do with me?

It's urgent, the voice says.

What? What do you mean? Who are you again?

Something about identifying human remains.

Her hand on her chest. She can't remember how to breathe.

Remains? Whose remains? What kind of sick joke is this?

They think it's her daughter.

Yes, my daughter is a teacher. She teaches children in Qatar.

Then she hears words, not complete sentences, but only disjointed words:

Burnt.

DNA.

Beyond identification.
Body.
Dental records.
Then the inexplicable eclipse. Her presence is required.
The lights go off.
Darkness takes over.

I imagine the look on her face at the Hamad Hospital Mortu-ary. Her disbelief. Her reluctance to accept that these charred remains are her daughter. Where is her face so she can kiss it? Where are her lips? Where did the eyes go? What happened to her legs? She thinks about walking away. She would refuse to identify the remains and would not leave the country until her real daughter, the whole of her, is returned. Then they would fly back to England, and that would be the end of it. What a cruel mishap to make her fly all the way there to identify the wrong body. But she can't identify her daughter, not just because she is grief-stricken and in denial, but because what was left of the body weighs only seven-and-a-half kilograms. As heavy as a gallon of paint. A Jack Russell. Three bricks. Her daughter is a collection of disassembled body parts: a chunk of her skull, a portion of her neck, the braces on her upper jaw teeth, a section of her chest with a twenty-centimeter knife still lodged in her ribs, and the feet, my God, the feet. They are intact, not through an act of mercy, but because the men had dumped her body head-first into the fire pit, sparing her feet from the flames. Her toenails are painted red. How odd. The mother recognizes the red nail polish. The weight on her chest is unbearable. She is all tremors and tears. She is disheveled and infinitely cold, so cold. She feels like screaming, like putting fists through walls, like tearing her clothes off, like putting her rapturous rage to good use. This mother, unhinged by grief, needs an explanation. She wants to know whose ribs she is looking at and who put the knife there. Such a vulgar anachronism. She wants to know who turned her daughter into this burnt changeling: a child stolen by desert spirits.

Since October 2013, sometimes I'd lay in bed and think of The English Teacher. I wonder if her bones made any sound as she burned in the pit. Did they crackle like dry twigs burning in a fire? Did they sound like autumn leaves crunched under one's weight? Like sparks, a Fourth of July of the body? I rely heavily on metaphors because I don't have the right words to describe a pain that's not mine. The desecration of a body I didn't bring to this world. The death of a young woman I never met. A phone call that I didn't receive. The language of emotion is too simple, the ABCs of being alive, to describe somebody else's pain. So, I resort to using figurative language, looking inside its vastness for the words I need to imagine the crime itself and the pain that ensued.

The newspapers didn't say much. They ran timid news on the crime, the only homicide in the country in several years, then stopped reporting. Life quickly returned to what it was before: activities at the souk, fashion shows, visiting diplomats, new restaurants, brand new hotels, lavish brunches, soft and grand shopping mall openings. So much to see and do. Better not to give the readers the wrong impression. After all, Qatar is considered one of the safest countries in the world. A nation with no history of bank robberies, muggings, break-ins, or stolen vehicles. No drug dealers ruining neighborhoods, drive-by shootings, or street gangs. Why destroy that outstanding record with gory details about a single crime? The country needs Western technology, foreign expertise, and English teachers. Let them come. No need to scare them away. This was an isolated event. There were almost eighteen thousand British citizens living in the country in 2013. One dead Briton out of eighteen thousand equals 0.0055 percent, all those invalidating zeros to the left.

The expat community spoke about it at coffee breaks and executive lunches. Over Friday bubbly and happy hour at the Ritz. Poor thing. Have you seen her Facebook page? All miniskirts and booze. Was he her boyfriend? Maybe she was pregnant, and that's why he killed her. I hope she didn't suffer. Oh God, I hope she was dead when they set her on fire. C'mon, she knew what she was doing when she got in the car with two Arab men. For God's sake, you don't wear a miniskirt in a Muslim country. Was she really wearing a miniskirt? Was she drunk? There you go. What do you expect?

Soon after the falconer discovered her body, both Arab men were apprehended. The Friend accepted a plea bargain—he pleaded guilty to aiding in disposing of her body and gave a full confession in exchange for three years behind bars—three years, the same sentence for a third DUI in Connecticut. The Friend's confession satisfied the jury. The men had driven The Teacher to an apartment. They drank. The Man took her into a room to have sex with her. The Friend didn't touch her, he claimed. Sometime later, The Man came out of the room in shock, begging his friend for help. He had stabbed The English Teacher twice. She was dead. They drove her body to the city's outskirts, dumped it into a pit near a farm, and set it ablaze.

"We tell ourselves stories in order to live," Joan Didion wrote. I think she meant we need answers, motives, and a life filled with meaningful moments. The wounded people—The Teacher's family and friends—and the rest of us want to know why. The tragedy is easier to understand if we know what caused it: lust, jealousy, hatred, revenge, or any other emotional tenor commensurate with the savagery of the act. His lawyers claimed self-defense. A 5'5" petite woman allegedly attacked a strong man towering over her, and he stabbed her in a fleeting bout of self-preservation. The defense argued at various times that he was mentally impaired at the time of the murder and that police had interrogated their client without a lawyer. On one occasion, the defense claimed that The Teacher had committed suicide.

The court refused to use the word "rape," and so did the local newspapers. It was reported that The Teacher had been "conquered." Conquered. The irony. She was raped and stabbed on October 12, the day Columbus conquered the New World. One could talk about Columbus's rape of America, but one could not talk about the conquest of The Teacher.

Semantics.

To conquer.

Origin: from Old French *conquerre*, based on Latin *conquirere* "gain, win," from con- an expression of completion + quaerere "seek."

Definition: To overcome and take control of (a place or people) by military force, as in China conquered Tibet. The Teacher was not conquered.

To successfully overcome (a problem or weakness), as in to conquer one's fears. The Teacher was not conquered.

To climb (a mountain) successfully, as in Edmund Hillary was the first Briton to conquer Everest. The Teacher was not conquered.

To gain the love, admiration, or respect for a person or group of people. No, no, and a thousand times no. The Teacher was not conquered.

Conquest: The act or process of conquering. The Teacher. This Woman. This Daughter was not his conquest.

A few years ago, I contacted The Teacher's mother. I was writing a chapter for a book about the repatriation of human remains and wanted to interview her. We met at a hotel, hugged lightly, looked into each other's eyes without mentioning her daughter, ordered tea, and talked about the weather, the traffic, her trips to appear in court—almost twenty, the ignominy of it all. How when she goes to court, she grabs a number and stands in a queue to be heard by a jury of men. How she has to stand there and listen as her interpreter translates everyone's grievances: a stolen laptop from someone's room in a work camp, a mobile phone left in a cab, a landlord increasing the rent beyond what's stipulated by the law, a work visa that can't be transferred, unpaid salaries, a poisoned dog, then her voice: My daughter was raped, stabbed to death, and set ablaze, your honor, followed by other pitiful grievances. It wasn't just the perversity of what had been done to her daughter. It was also the humiliation of the circus-like court proceedings. There was the reenactment of the crime for which she flew in. In the recreation, The Teacher was played by a male actor. She raged in silence. The prosecution complained. The scene showed two men of about the same height and weight scuffling. It didn't represent the disparity in size and weight between The Man and The Teacher. A new hearing was scheduled, and she flew back home. Later she flew back to Doha for the "real" reenactment. The same movie was shown in court. No new reenactment had been produced. She went back to the UK, deflated, humiliated but undeterred. She came back for another showing. This time due to technical difficulties, no audiovisual equipment was available, and a tiny laptop had to be brought in for the jury. Unfortunately, the laptop had run out of power, and the lead was not long enough to reach the socket from the juror's table. She had to go home with no answers. A few months later, she bought another round-trip ticket to Qatar. For the umpteenth time, she went home empty-handed and again and again ad infinitum.

I didn't want to sound trite. What I wanted was to have the ability to offer her something substantial, not another I'm sorry for your loss, although I was, and still am, terribly sorry for her loss. What I wanted was an impossibility: to have the power to save her the indignity of standing in line as if her daughter's murder was another petty misdemeanor, to have this solution she hadn't thought of, the *wasta*, influence, to expedite the process and give her the only thing close to closure: The Man's execution. But I had nothing of value to offer. Instead, I asked imprudent questions about the repatriation of her daughter's remains. She gave me nothing. Afraid of interfering with the process, she had stopped talking to the press or anyone out-side family and friends—a self-imposed gag order of sorts. We hugged goodbye, and I watched her walk away. It hurt to watch the fluency of a body acclimated to grief.

I can't get this young woman out of my mind. When I'm not thinking about her last minutes, I think about her mom. Some-times I even think of the other grieving mother. The Man is somebody else's son. There was another heartbroken mother on the other side of the courtroom. Another mother looking at her child and praying for leniency, for another year, one more Ra-madan, one more Eid, a mother fighting for his life. The irony is that The Teacher's mother doesn't want The Man to die either. She'd much rather see him get old behind bars, have the certain-ty that he will never see the sunrise again. But that's not a choice. She either forgives him—and he walks—or she doesn't—and he gets the death penalty. On a few occasions during the hearings, The Teacher's mother crossed paths with The Man as she came out of the restroom. She looked into his dark eyes, the same pair of eyes her daughter must have stared into as he raped her and later while he drove the knife beyond her skin as if looking for her heart. The amount of self-restraint it must have taken her to look at him and not attack him. What mantras did she repeat in her head to keep her fingernails from scratching the skin on his face or gouging his eyes? How hard did she bite her tongue and bleed inside the mouth to drown all the expletives she knew, to not spit her fury on the chest guarding his still-beating heart?

The outlandish defense arguments didn't hold any water. In 2014, he was sentenced to death. In 2015, his death sentence was upheld. In 2016, after countless court hearings, his ruling was overturned, the verdict was thrown out, and a retrial began. In 2017, a judge asked The Teacher's mother whether she wanted to forgive or seek financial retribution against her daughter's rapist and killer. No, she didn't want to forgive him, and no, she didn't want blood money. The Man was sentenced to death for the second time, which was to be carried out by firing squad or hanging. I wonder if she had any preference. Then came 2018, The Teacher's mother made her trip number 30 to Qatar to attend Judgment Day and hear from the judge's mouth when the death sentence would be carried out. Only, the defense team had appealed again and had managed to get his death sentence reduced to ten years in jail.

He has already served five.

He'll be out after Qatar hosts the 2022 World Cup.

Sometimes I lay in bed and think of everything I had the chance to tell The Teacher's mother when we met, but didn't. How I met her hoping to get something from her when I should have given her something, although I still don't know what I'd offer to a mother who had lost a child other than a litany of impossibilities.

Dear Mrs. Patterson,

You are not alone. It only feels that way. There is a large, rowdy tribe of women hungry for justice for Lauren. Nothing will take away the pain; no one will replace your daughter, and not a day will go by that you don't wish she were alive, but life will go on. Inexplicably. Stubbornly. The sun will rise every morning, and with it, the promise of blue skies, dewdrops, tides, and rain, which means butterflies, bees, trees, flowers, and rivers. The ugly stuff, too, of course. Sandstorms, floods, volcanic eruptions, destruction, death. Your grief won't stop your neighbor's kids from laughing outside or your friends from having sex. Despite the vulgarity of our quotidian lives, there will be Christmases and stores sales, books and songs will be written, the animal kingdom will continue to birth more humans and more animals, which is both reassuring and terrifying. And when the earth's rotational cycle is all over, the sun will rise again, and yes, you will have no option but to make the best of that single day without her. You will have no option but to make it all the way to nightfall, and whether you do this on your knees or your feet, it's up to you.

Every mother who gives birth to a daughter holds dual citizenship: one in the kingdom of her own womb, which is sacred but limited to a few months, where the daughter is queen, and one in the kingdom of the world, which is mysterious, dangerous, dissonant, and finite, where the daughter is nothing but a grain of sand. You will move back and forth between the two kingdoms, the twenty-four-year span when she was a hug and a kiss away. And this space between fury and despair will eventually be filled with love. The kind that comes at you like an uninvited guest and leaves you trembling with gratitude. Love like jazz riffs, sharp and pungent one minute, wary and saccharine the next. Life will go on, Mrs. Patterson. For you, for me, and for every woman who gives birth or is birthed into this world so that we can crystallize our dreams of equality, safety, and justice. This much I know.

15

Three Women

She walks into the fancy part of a shopping mall wearing a matching set of Louis Vuitton high heels and a handbag. Her abaya is wide open at the front, exposing a black turtleneck maxi dress that screams wealth. An animal print scarf around her head—the words Dolce & Gabbana printed in one corner—and a pair of the oversized 1.1 Millionaires sunglasses made to evoke Al Capone's Chicago complement her ensemble. She holds the S-lock hinges of her sunglasses with her gloved hands and sets them on her head atop the silk scarf. I don't know why she wears black gloves and sunglasses inside the mall. Or wears heavy makeup and those impossibly heavy fake eyelashes that make every wink appear like an irreversible move. I suspect these items are class markers, indicators that she is a member of the local elite, a little something that sets her apart from other women, even though other women in the same shopping mall wear similar attire and makeup. This is a wealthy country. It's hard to stand out as an affluent citizen when everyone in your circle has access to similar wealth. There she is, the chain of her monogrammed bag in the nook of her elbow as she answers her phone. Her face contorts with exasperation first, then with something close to anger. She is upset about something. The woman moves her free hand up in the air, twisting like she is screwing in a light bulb. I know the sign. She is asking why, why, why not? Whatever she hears over the phone seems to soothe her, her anger subsidies. She smiles for everyone to see a set of unnaturally white teeth so conspicuous that they put all the white in the world to shame—snow, and glaciers and clouds and cotton fields and vanilla ice creams. She finds her reflection in a window and fixes her headscarf with her free hand. She seems to like what she sees. The woman puckers her tragically pumped lips, making me think of platypuses and Donald Duck, as she walks on.

A few feet behind her walks a short woman in a baby blue uniform like the scrubs nursing students wear. She is not a nurse, though. At least not in this country, where she has been hired to babysit these two children, one of whom is having a meltdown. He kicks her shins because his mom is too busy on the phone while he is stuck with this Filipina maid who smells of garlic and ginger, unlike mom's Mon Guerlain Eau de Parfum. The maid, who has neither the power nor the language to quell his mighty tantrum, endures his abuse in silence. She kneels in front of this three-foot-tall tyrant and says gently, La, la, la, habibi, no, no, no honey, and I wonder if she is thinking of her well-behaved children left in the Philippines to be raised by their grandma. How she taught them to say yes, please, and thank you, ma'am. How they would never behave like these two children under her care. How, if she had them in front of her right now, they'd have their tiny arms around her neck, covering her face with kisses that taste like sweet plantain candy, instead of kicking and slapping her legs with hands that haven't been taught control or self-sufficiency because there is no need to teach dexterity in a world where Filipina maids turn every whim into reality.

Ten thousand miles away, a grandmother is tending to her grandchildren. They look like her daughter, who works in Qatar as a nanny. Thank God they don't look like their good-for-nothing father who ran away after the second child was born. That's why the children are there with Grandma, crammed in a slum in Mindanao, eating what she can buy with the money her daughter sends religiously every month to the Western Union three blocks down a sad strip littered with plastic bottles and stray dogs. Life in Qatar is good, her daughter says. Her madam is a genuinely lovely person. The children whom she babysits adore her. They are so well-behaved. She doesn't have to cook or clean; that's for the maids (plural) of the house, the poor souls. She is a nanny, three notches above a maid. Every night, she sings Tagalog lullabies to the two cherubs until they fall asleep in her arms; then, she lovingly places them in their respective beds. Like Mary Poppins? the nanny's mom asks over the phone. Better than Mary Poppins. She doesn't have to wear that silly hat or carry a stupid umbrella. Much better than Mary Poppins. Life in Qatar is a dream come true. The grandmother has questions, many questions, but chooses not to ask. Sometimes faith in the potential of a fantasy, no matter how farfetched, is all you need to get you through the night.

They sit at two tables in a French restaurant next to the shopping mall's food court—the elegant woman and her children here, the nanny close by, but still over there. The children are hungry. They order chicken nuggets, french fries, and icy Coca-Colas, items readily available next door in the food court at a fraction of the price, but not as nicely presented. The elegant woman orders soup and a salad, neither of which seems to please her. She leaves them on the table untouched, along with a basket of French pastries and a cappuccino. The nanny's table is clean, not wiped-with-Windex clean, but empty. There is no food on her table—only a few shopping bags with designers' names embossed on them. I don't know why she is not eating. Maybe there is a contractual understanding that maids don't eat at French restaurants with their employers. Maybe she'd rather eat the food she is familiar with—rice and shredded chicken—and French cuisine is wasted on her. Maybe she'll eat chicken nuggets and french fries later in the food court. Maybe she won't be offered anything to eat at all.

She sits there in silence, her eyes fixated on the kids, at the ready should they want anything from her—to wipe their noses, take them to the restroom, offer them her shins for a bit of kicking, take them by their sticky hands to the ice cream stall while mom reapplies her mascara.

The previous night was rough. If I could see the woman's hands under the gloves, I'd see a bruise on her right forearm and four red and blue lines around her left wrist, one per each angry finger. Her husband got mad about something she couldn't pinpoint. It could have been the price of the sunglasses she is wearing today, or the hours she was on the phone texting her girlfriends, or the Zumba class she took at a posh gym, which he explicitly forbade her to attend because dancing in skintight leggings leaves nothing to the imagination, even though it is a ladies-only class. But it's not her spending, texting, or working out that awakens his wrath. What sets his heart ablaze is the knowledge that she can find pleasure away from him. It's the knowledge that something he can't control excites her and makes her smile and feel alive. His wrath is unpredictable. It is a desert jinni that attacks and leaves guerrilla-style. Sometimes it is the way she smiles, or the color of her lipstick, or a joke she doesn't get, or the way she treats his body in bed, like an unwanted guest, a relative who drops by unexpectedly and who she is obliged to be nice to, but wants gone as soon as he arrives. Yes, he gets rough. Yes, he forces himself on her. Thank God it's not rape. Thank God husbands can't rape their wives. It's a known fact.

The nanny is not a nanny. The nanny is their maid, their cook, their childminder, and the recipient of her madam's frustration, which is random, heavy, and icy, like a hailstorm. Sometimes it is a downpour of insults. She calls her helper names the helper doesn't understand because she doesn't speak enough Arabic to decipher the verbal onslaught. Sometimes the employer throws in a few insults in English, which the nanny/cook/maid understands slightly better: stupid, idiot, useless, ugly, words she learned from watching American TV in the Philippines. Some other times it's a push and a shove, symbolic attempts at making the nanny disappear, to move her out of her field of vision and into the ether. Some days the boss's anger comes in the form of hair-pulling and a slap on the back of her head. Reproachable, humiliating, unbearable, yet nothing, *nothing*, compares to her madam's silent treatment. The days the Filipina wakes up and no one talks to her are the worst. She doesn't know what to cook, where to clean, or whether the children want Fruity Loops or Cocoa Pops. It's the days when she is not acknowledged that hurt the most. It's the wondering, the constant dithering, the walking around the house like she is defusing a bomb bound to go off at any time. Those are the days when she feels the farthest away from home, isolated, forgotten, invisible. First thing in the morning, right after the first call to prayer, she walks into the kitchen to fix her employer some karak tea, and even though everything is in its appointed place, just like she left it four hours earlier before she went to bed, she can't find her way around. The loose black tea is in its pretty tin box, and the cardamom is crushed and aromatic. The condensed milk has the right viscosity, the cinnamon, saffron, ginger, the cloves, all of it exactly where it is supposed to be; yet, this kitchen, bigger than her mom's house in Mindanao, is unknown territory. On these days, when her boss is in a foul mood and refuses to talk, the helper doesn't pray for comfort, money, gratitude, or sleep; she just wants to feel alive. A slap on the back of her head or an insult—aha, you are here—would be better than silence.

It's not a bad life by any stretch of the imagination, she reasons as she sips her karak. Her husband owns a house in Marbella and an apartment in London. They have money and a family name that makes people move out of their way. They drive luxury cars and wear expensive jewelry and designer clothes. They have a gardener, a driver, and a maid. He is in the import business, wait, or is it export? He is faithful, a good father, an exemplary son, and a good husband. He's got a bit of a temper—you can't ask for a perfect husband—a fuse short and capricious—hey, she can be a real pain too—but he is a good Muslim man. And it doesn't enter her head that maybe the two are incompatible. It doesn't dawn on her that a man cannot claim allegiance to a higher power five times a day and rough his wife up between prayer calls. That a good man, Muslim or not, doesn't lay a finger on a woman, doesn't force himself on her, doesn't treat her like a possession.

The maid's room is smaller than the children's bathroom and slightly bigger than their closet.

The maid's room has a tiny window that doesn't open, an AC unit that doesn't work, a floor fan that wobbles, a twin bed in desperate need of a new mattress, and a restroom without a door—a deterrent to discourage maids from taking long showers.

The maid's room is next to the kitchen. In the kitchen, there is a multi-door refrigerator.

The refrigerator has a lock and a key—a deterrent to hungry maids who wander in the middle of the night looking for nourishment.

The maid has health insurance (it's the law) but doesn't know how to make a doctor's appointment or where the health centers are.

The maid has Fridays off. Health centers are closed on Fridays.

The maid has a contract written in Arabic. She doesn't know what it says but hopes she'll get paid as much as she was promised by the employment agency. Maybe she'll call the Filipino embassy on her day off. The embassies are closed on Fridays.

The maid had heard stories before she left Mindanao. She wrote the embassy's number in pencil on the last page of her newly issued passport. You never know.

The maid's employer confiscated the passport upon her arrival—a deterrent to maids who want to quit their jobs and abscond.

It's not a bad life at all, she reasons, as she valets her SUV in the Ritz Hotel, where she is meeting two cousins for high tea. She is not like her maternal grandmother, who was married off to a man twice her age when she was fifteen. How awful. Or like her paternal grandmother who had to wear the battoulah, a metallic-looking burqa made of leather, a contraption that left a permanent mark on her nose where the material rubbed her skin for decades. How provincial. She is a modern woman. She chose her husband, wears the abaya and the hijab because she wants to, she comes and goes without a chaperone, has her own credit card, and stopped having children because one girl and one boy are all she ever wanted. She is not like both her grandmothers who fetched water from wells, gave birth on woven sheep wool rugs, had a few miscarriages and a few stillbirths. Yet all those who thrived in the inclement Qatari weather are the fabric of a family so big and close-knit that makes friendships with outsiders redundant. Plus, outsiders don't understand the local culture. They come with funny ideas that work in their part of the world but not here. Like conjugal rape. How ridiculous. If she wants to know anything, *anything*, she asks her cousins. And her cousins give her the answers they have extracted from television, movies, schoolmates, and other cousins. Life is that simple. Alhamdulillah, praise be to God.

The maid, who is not a maid but a registered nurse, built her Middle East dream on pictures. From her cousin, Chubby Rosa, who works in Kuwait and bombards friends and family in the Philippines with shots of herself sporting sunglasses and knockoff designer jeans, she learned that Kuwait compensates heftily Filipino labor. Chubby Rosa has lost weight. When she pouts for the camera with arms akimbo, head tilted to one side, and the impossibly green Persian Gulf as the backdrop, she is the epitome of upward mobility. Lisa, the maid's neighbor in Mindanao, left the country to look after a rich Saudi elder in Riyad. Lisa favors pictures of glitzy shopping malls, swanky hotels, and sports cars over selfies. She tells the maid who is not a maid that Saudi Arabia is not as bad a country as shown on TV. If you work hard, she told her in a letter, you make a lot of money, especially if you have a "generous" boss. The maid ignored the emphasis on "generous." From Auntie Elma, who stopped sending pictures a few months after she arrived in the Emirates over a decade ago, hasn't seen her children in all these years, and has never missed a monthly money transfer to the nearest Western Union to pay for her children's universities in Manila, the maid who is not a maid but a registered nurse learned that leaving children behind in the care of relatives to work abroad is the only way to guarantee their survival. She suspected that the lives she saw in these pictures were too good to be true, but a dream is better than nothing. A mirage gives one something to swim toward. Even in the desert.

Naturally, when the recruiter showed up in Mindanao advertising jobs in the Middle East, she didn't think twice. She was in luck, the recruiter told her. There was significant demand for nurses in Qatar. She applied for sponsorship—the only way to obtain gainful employment in the Gulf countries—paid the recruiter a hefty fee, a practice she didn't know was illegal, and said goodbye to her two children. She would work as a nurse in a wealthy country with a king, princesses, and royal palaces. That night, the maid and her mom lit candles to all the Catholic saints they knew. *Salamat sa Diyos.* Their humble home looked like a sad nativity set. Life would be better. In a few months, the house will have proper plumbing, and the children will have their own bedrooms. Their debts will be paid off, and there will be money for windows, a bathroom with a shower, and a little garden. *Salamat sa Diyos* for this opportunity.

Two weeks later, she landed at Qatar International Airport, her entry paperwork written in Arabic. Profession: maid.

Naturally, soon after her arrival, she starts sending pictures back home. First on the corniche—the iconic waterfront promenade extending for seven kilometers along Doha Bay—where she strikes her best poses for the camera. The immensity of the aquamarine Persian Gulf behind her swallows her whole. Her five-foot frame, her lustrous long black hair, the dimples framing her smile, her broad face, her light skin, and the fantastic Qatari Riviera make a perfect publicity poster. Come to Qatar, where your Filipino dreams crystallize. Plastic sunglasses on, snap. Wind whipping her hair, snap. Legs crossed at the ankle, snap. Snap, snap, snap until the sun comes down because sunsets make the people in the picture look as if they are on holiday. She sends her mom and children the best shots with a caption in Tagalog, *ang buhay ay maganda*, life is beautiful.

Naturally, her mom shares the pictures with everyone on her phone's contact list. Her daughter looks much happier than Chubby Rosa, Lisa, and Elma put together. She tells her granddaughter that she, too, can go to the Middle East when she grows up and live like a princess, just like mom. And she tells her own sisters, a couple of neighbors, and women from the church they should send their daughters too. Maybe in a year or two, she will be able to have a second floor built as Auntie Elma did, only Elma has never seen it. Maybe she won't have to wait that long if her daughter, the nanny, gets a salary raise. Two hundred American dollars per month goes a long way in Mindanao.

Naturally, other women start thinking about migrating to the Middle East, although the thought prevails: the pictures look too good to be true. They have also heard stories. But life goes on; they get pregnant, only a few men stick around, and being a single mom in Mindanao is so hard. They allow themselves to dream. Sometimes a dream is better than nothing. A mirage gives one something to swim toward. Even in the desert.

That's the thing about life. It goes on everywhere. There is a worldwide pandemic, Qatar is on lockdown, and the maid hasn't been allowed to leave the house. The place that used to feel expansive and unfillable with its bare walls, long corridors, sky-high ceilings, and empty landings is now oppressive. She hasn't been able to send any money home since the beginning of the lockdown, three months now. The Western Union office is closed, and her salary is rapidly shrinking. Every month she gets a little bit less. She doesn't ask why because she knows of other Filipina maids in worse condition than hers. The maid service agencies have shut down, home cleaning services are forbidden, and with nothing to sweep/mop/dust off, the day laborers who clean houses, schools, offices are stuck in their accommodations—four to a room. There is no income without work; there is no money to wire home without pay. The airport is closed. There are no repatriation flights to the Philippines. These maids' lives hang by a thread. No, the nanny who is not a nanny but a maid doesn't say anything. She is lucky she has a roof over her head. She'll wait until the pandemic is over.

That's the thing about pandemics, such equalizers. The lady of the house is packing on the pounds now that the gyms are closed. His import business, or is it export, has come to a complete halt.

He spends his days drinking tea and smoking shisha in his majlis, his Qatari version of a mancave with carpets on the floor and cushions against the walls. The confinement has shortened his fuse. They've had a couple of rows, one of which ended with his hands around her porcelain neck. She is not considering a divorce, though. Under sharia law, she'd lose custody of her children, and without them, she is nothing. In any case, the women in her family, and his, don't divorce their husbands. They endure marriage like their ancestors survived the desert, with chests puffed up and hope in the Almighty until their skin hardened and their feet grew calloused. Until they learned to feel nothing but hunger, thirst, and the universal tug below the belly.

That's the thing about repetition; it confuses the brain. The recurrence of an action, or inaction, becomes a pattern. A pattern becomes a method. A method sanctions the recurrence. Before you know it, this lying around smoking and drinking tea all day becomes a lifestyle; waking up at noon (there is nowhere to go), binge-watching Netflix all night, replacing the Zumba classes with tubs of Ben and Jerry's, allowing the children unlimited time on their iPads, watching the hours go by, wishing for this craziness to end, hoping, praying, sleeping, ad infinitum becomes acceptable. She is depressed. He is depressed. The maid is depressed. The grandmother in Mindanao is depressed—the new normal.

That's the thing about silence, so versatile, so accommodating, and so easy to get lost in its vastness. She doesn't say anything because he won't listen, because he has become aloof and impossible to read, because he doesn't care, because he no longer speaks her language, because he is incapable of walking in her direction to meet her halfway. He doesn't say anything because she doesn't know that although they don't need money, it is his business that defines him. That being on the phone, breaking deals, buying, and selling gives him status, and without that, he feels emasculated. The maid doesn't ask why she is not receiving her full salary, doesn't tell her employers that in July the temperature in her room reached 120° F, or that she is a nurse, *a nurse*, not a maid. She doesn't tell her mom that life is unbearable in Qatar, that everyone treats her like she is a couch—something whose only function is to quietly exist in one corner of the house. She doesn't tell her mom that she misses Tagalog, her mother tongue, like she misses her children. That she misses her children the way she misses the woman she was before Qatar. That life has lost its pulse. That sometimes she wakes up and feels nothing. Nothing. The grandmother thinks that it might be better if her daughter comes back home until the pandemic is under control but doesn't say anything. It'd be cruel to ask her daughter to give up her dream. She wants her daughter to be happy, as happy as she is, even if she is 4,500 miles away.

Life goes on.

She starts taking antidepressants but doesn't tell anyone. The day after he choked her, she considered taking the whole bottle. She didn't.

The maid makes a noose with a jump rope she found among the children's toys. She doesn't use it. She just stares at it and ponders the weight it would hold.

Her mother in Mindanao lights more candles, not out of devotion, but because the electricity was shut off.

The women go to bed in different rooms, beds, time zones, and dream dreams that are forbidden, criminal, lustful, stupid, incomprehensible, simple, and when they wake up, they tell no one where their hearts have been.

16

Dear Julie,

We are inside the yoga studio where I teach. After one hour of restorative poses, I ask the women attending class to lay their heads on a soft cushion and place a ten-pound sandbag across their pelvises. I go around distributing heavy Mexican blankets. I want them to swaddle themselves, make a cocoon, block the light with a lavender-infused eye pillow, and rest in Savasana—corpse pose. The studio grows quiet. Everyone surrenders in complete stillness to their yoga mats, like milk spilled over marble. The AC units have been off for the entire class, but a phantom whirr fills the room.

I go from yoga mat to yoga mat, tending to everyone until I get to you. I unfold a Mexican blanket and tuck you in as if we were my child.

I soak my hands in Navratna oil. I let its nine Indian herbs soak my palms and fingers, rub my hands vigorously to generate heat, place them above your nose, and let you inhale the oil to signal that I'm about to lay hands on your head. I start small and light as if asking for your permission to proceed. I place my thumbs right at the center of your forehead and press your temples with the remaining fingers. I press and release. Move the thumbs to the birth of your eyebrows. Press and release. I walk my thumbs toward the outer edges of your brows. Press and release. The oil smells of eucalyptus and flowers, of sticks and shrubs, of smoke and cinnamon. I pray the scent will keep you grounded. Right here, on the mat, hearing each other's breaths.

I study your face as I move my oil-soaked hands toward your neck. Your lips quiver lightly, a sleepy infant about to have a meltdown. When I say your lips quiver, I mean now. Not too long ago, you'd firmly press them together as if making a tight knot, your personal black box, a woman attempting to stop her sobs from alarming everyone around her. Who taught you to cry that hard without making a sound? Who told you that silence was your best friend, the most loyal ally a little girl could ask for?

You were born the first time you broke your forty-year-long silence. A woman in her fifties just beginning to live. The day you broke your silence was the day you stopped your ongoing self-annihilation. You said the words, and they sounded like the first words you had ever said. A middle-aged woman all her life communicating with the world in shorthand and smoke signals. And because this was the first time you spoke about the scars on your body, the nightmares, the impulses, the irrational way in which silence had dictated your existence, it was also the first time you felt seen. I understood that you had lived all your life in a perpetual state of mourning. I understood your rough edges and how grief has its uncanny way of molding a woman's face. I understood your frown, the ridges in the corners of your mouth, your hands curled into fists on the yoga mat, the grief over the childhood you were robbed of, and everything written on your face.

And that's why you cry when I touch you in yoga class.

You inhale the eucalyptus. Your breathing changes from that frantic staccato—its native language—to a succession of deep, controlled ins and outs. I knead the soft flesh of your nape with my fingertips. I infuse my love into you. I command my fingers to transmit more than physical comfort into your being. I distribute my fingertips evenly around your skull and make tiny circles, hard tiny, soft tiny, strands of your gray hair stuck to my oily hands until the circles get bigger and bigger and concentric, and my fingers so intent that it feels as though they are talking to you.

Dear Julie, don't be alarmed by my touch or the heat on your scalp. I'm always warm. Let all the Indian sages in this oil exorcise your demons; let me in. I mean no harm. Open your heart until it beats in perfect synch with mine until neither of us can tell them apart—your heart and mine. I'm going to hold you tight until the memories of the monster who destroyed your life fade into the mat, until the unspoken, unnamed, concealed anger in you disappears like smoke. Let me be the sister you never had. Let me be a better mother than the one who turned a blind eye to your suffering. Let me be your partner in crime, and when I say crime, I mean it in every sense of the word.

Let's Kill Your Grandfather Together.

Let's startle him from his forbidden dreams with strident bugles, dissonant bagpipes, pots, and pans clattering on one another. Let's cut off his electricity so when he rouses from his dream of you, panting with confusion, and reaches for the light switch, there is nothing but darkness all around him, and he won't know how his wet dream of a blond little girl turned into this unbearable nightmare.

Let's offer him the candy he likes, you, and lure him to the garden shed behind your grandmother's house. When we get him there, while he licks his whiskers, a lion slobbering over his bleeding prey, strike him down with the same iron rod he soaked in your blood forty years ago.

Let's not kill him just yet. For now, let's infuse his blue veins with a paralyzer and put him in a trance so that he can watch and feel but not move as we peel off shards of every inch of his leathery skin that ever touched you. Then mix it with salt and feed it to the dog you were so afraid of.

Let's tie your blond braids in knots around his neck while we sip champagne and watch him silently turn blue until his heart nearly stops. Then we will loosen the knot and let him live, only to do it all over again and again. A taste of his own medicine.

The agony he put you through every Sunday before swimming practice.

Let's take him to the top of the 22 Bishopsgate Tower, the highest skyscraper in London, and offer half of his body to the void, let him see the drop, let fear burn his eyes like cigarettes, let him scream words of repentance and beg for your forgiveness. Then you'll say, "No, Grandfather, too late, not enough," push him further off and let him dangle by the shoelaces of his filthy boots.

Let's put him on all fours, against the wall, bent and humiliated over the workbench he kept in his shed, and enter him with rage, with acid and sand, with wild eyes. Let him hear you scream all the screams you stifled under his command. Force his jaws wide open, the way he did yours every Sunday, dislodge them, make them crack like twigs in the fire until his throat burns with the flames of his own bile. I will be there, still rubbing Navratna oil on your nape. And I won't let up until he dies in your head. Until we both kill him with the sheer power of our embrace.

Let's walk out of the shed, face the dog that terrified you, and show him no fear. Give him commands. Sit. Roll over. Give me a paw. Good boy. March on without giving him a treat.

Let's make a hole in the garden to bury them both and their ghosts. And while we dig, look at your mother and grandmother through the window. They had been sipping tea while their father and husband desecrated your body. Ask your mother why. Why? Why? Whack the window with the shovel, with your hands, with your braids dripping chlorine, with your blood-soaked swimming suit. Why? And watch your mother turn to look at your grandmother, asking her with pleading eyes the same question. Why, Mom? Why? Their individual and compound silences will be the only explanation you will ever get. Your hunch that many girls' cries have silently howled into the night for three generations will be your only answer.

I tap your hands lightly to remind you to let go of the fists. There is no one to fight off here. It's just us on yoga mats. I look at the wall clock—time to wrap up the class. I bring everyone back from their slumber with soothing, reassuring words. You are safe here, and all is well. Slowly the women get up, roll their yoga mats, return the props, and hug one another. We are a tribe of war veterans, soldiers of life, sweet, triumphant warriors with prolapsed bladders, extra pounds here and there, age moles in all the wrong places, a few wrinkles, and gray hair. I hug you goodbye. See you next class, I say. What I don't say is that in my mind, I have just avenged you. I don't tell you about the violence I committed while you surrendered your head to my palms. I couldn't. This is your pain, your wound, your scar, your cage. Not mine. This is neither my journey nor my fight to fight. It's all yours. All I can do is watch you swim to the other side of pain and cheer you on.

Dear Julie, the next time the memory of him assaults you again in your dreams, at the grocery store, on the beach, under the sheets when you're with your husband, breathe the way I have taught you in class, with an active diaphragm and quiet chest. Inhale with a big belly, hold, and exhale with a loud sigh. Let him and his ghost go.

The monster of your girlhood has been dead for decades.

Go to sleep without looking for him under your bed, in your closet, or behind every door.

The only thing left of him is in your head.

Go to sleep. You don't have to keep quiet anymore. Forty years of silence is too heavy a cross for a tiny woman like you.

Go to sleep.

You have spoken now. You no longer are under the old man's spell.

You are safe now, and all will be well.

Letter to a Younger Self

Dear twenty-six-year-old self,

In the picture, you look radiant in the way anorexic models look radiant on the catwalk. You are all skin and bones. At twenty-six, you weigh less than a hundred pounds, but donning this ivory-colored skirt and corset ensemble you paid for with the overdraft on your credit card, you are the epitome of chic. The bonnet veil is tilted, and as you turn around to face the camera, the sunrays make your fabulous black hair sparkle. You look deceivingly gorgeous. Behind you is Caesar's Palace, and in front of you is a white stretch limousine, its back door open for you. If all the pomposity around you makes you feel smug, like you have one on everyone who warned you against this very moment, you are tragically wrong, sweetheart. Don't get into the limo. Don't let the driver take your sad wedding party of four to the We've Only Just Begun Wedding Chapel located in the Imperial Palace hotel-casino. It's on the Las Vegas Strip, surrounded by drunk tourists, gamblers, and Johns, for goodness' sake. It's a place where, if you want, an Elvis Presley impersonator can officiate your wedding for twenty bucks, where the ministers perform four hundred and fifty weddings per day. Phony vow after phony vow. Don't say *I do* just because the cigarette burn on your wrist has already healed, or because the last time he slapped you, it wasn't so bad, or because he is good in the sack.

Here are the things you stand to lose if you say *I do.*

1. Your job. Forget about promotions, pay raises, and seminars abroad. Your new husband will desert you emotionally, financially, and physically, leaving you with nothing but low self-esteem and the conviction that you are not good at anything—a waste of space. A disposable little knick-knack that he stumbled upon while exploring your third-world country. A dirty Pocahontas doll that's lost its worth.

You stop caring. You don't think about your health, your personal appearance, or your job, which is to say, your only source of income. You sleep in, arrive late at work, leave early, call in sick, then you stop going to the office altogether. Nobody calls to check on you. Your irrelevance doesn't surprise you. He will have drilled it into your core: you are a third-world-country joke of a woman, you are stupid, you are nothing. He will convince you of your own worthlessness. You drink more to forget your insignificance. Your ex, who is also your mentor at work, your colleague, your boss, a step up an imaginary ladder, will have made it official in the office: you are a drunken whore. That's why he divorced you; that's why you don't go to work anymore. Naturally, his office groupies will believe him. Eventually, you will quit your job. There will be no farewell party for you: the first Colombian woman petroleum engineer-cum-geophysicist in the World Trade Center in Bogotá. Such a waste!

2. Your friends. And I'm using the word *friends* very lightly here, as you only have a few. Your life has revolved around this English man. At some point, you decided that he was your sun, and you were just one of the many barren planets barely existing in the periphery of its orbit. You have coworkers, Colombian oil-executive wannabes who would sell their mothers to eat the expensive sandwiches from the newly opened deli on the ground floor of the World Trade Center, which only the British bigwigs can afford. And because they are loyal to their wannabe essence, your *friends* will side with your English spouse when he sets out to destroy you. Your coworker Connie will be the only one by your side. Don't mistreat her. She is your only friend.

3. Your daughter. After the brief honeymoon, your marriage will collapse, starting a chain of implosions, explosions, and avalanches in varying degrees. You will soon discover that the dystopian world your life has become is easier to navigate after a bottle of red wine, sometimes midweek after work, occasionally first thing in the morning on weekends. Your baby girl from a previous failed marriage is five and more aware of the mess you are than you think. Putting her to bed an hour earlier so you can drink yourself to sleep without being seen won't help. She'll wake up in the middle of the night and see the bottles, the cigarette butts, you: a red-faced mommy choking in her own mommy sobs. Hear me out: reversing the process, getting hammered before bedtime, and then slurring lullabies into her innocent ears will not make you Mother of the Year. Stopping at a bar after work, having one too many, then picking her up from nursing school, sitting her in the back of your beat-up Fiat 147 with a gaping hole in the floor and no seatbelts, and driving home drunk doesn't make you badass. It makes you an incompetent mother, unworthy of that baby girl's love who thinks the world of you.

4. Your worth. At the unavoidable annulment of your Las Vegas marriage, the lawyer will ask you if you want spousal alimony. Al-*uh*-moh-nee. Your soon-to-be ex looks at you from across the table, his hands open to the sky. Well? he asks, his cold blue eyes piercing your soul, his voice jagged with impatience. Listen, sweetheart, you won't understand half of what will be said in your own divorce proceedings. You will stare at something on the floor, pretending to be thinking of an answer but secretly wondering about the meaning of the word alimony. English is so tricky. You'll shake your head no and walk out of the lawyer's office broke and heartbroken. You have left your Fiat at home because you can't bear the humiliation of letting him see the wreck you drive. After everything is said and done, you will stand in a corner to hail a cab, but it's raining, and no cabs will come your way. Your makeup will be smeared under the rain, and your hair, pristinely blow-dried a few minutes earlier, will be a limp tangle of shampoo, conditioner, and olive oil. Your high

heels will disappear in a muddy puddle of stagnant water. Planted in that corner, a 5'5" monument to sadness, you will take stock of your life. You no longer have a husband or a house with a garden; you are about to lose your job and the monthly checks that came with it. You are financially and spiritually shattered. You move into an efficiency where no one is waiting for you. Although you are not right in the head, in a fleeting moment of clarity, you sent your baby girl to be with your mom to spare her the carnage. This is the loneliest you will have been.

5. Your life. Your body will ache from too much alcohol, too many cigarettes, and too little food. You will switch your sad-looking twelve-inch TV on and watch Whitney Houston belt out "I Will Always Love You." In the video, Whitney, a woman of color, can't be with the love of her life, Kevin Costner, a white man. You will deem this the parallel perfect. Stop it. There is no parallel, sweetheart, and whatever it is you see, it's not perfect. He is an actor, a terrible actor, and they are not in love in real life. Just like what you two have is not love. Remember your childhood Bible, 1 Corinthians 13:

Love is patient, love is kind. It does not envy, it does not boast, it is not proud. It is not rude, it is not self-seeking, it is not easily angered, it keeps no record of wrongs.

Love does not delight in evil but rejoices with the truth. It always protects, always trusts, always hopes, always perseveres.

But you will be too intoxicated to see the truth. You will kneel in front of the TV and touch Whitney's lips on the screen as she sings that even though both know that she is not what he needs, she will always love him. Youuuuu. And somehow, in your warped perception of reality, you'll blame yourself for the demise of your relationship. And you will cry until your insides hurt, until your mouth goes so dry and your tongue so pasty that you won't be able to swallow your own saliva. And you will heave and wail in a cacophony of animal sounds; you will crawl on the dirty carpet you haven't vacuumed in weeks until you are in front of the mirror, and the mirror won't lie, baby. A skinny brown woman with deep dark circles under her eyes, matted hair, and colorless lips will stare at you. You will look deranged. You will touch the bruises on your face, the reminders of that last night together when you roughed, beat, slapped, shoe-heeled, or punched each other up—you won't remember—and think, it doesn't look too bad. You will open another bottle of Casillero del Diablo, drink half, get behind the wheel, the opened bottle wedged against the handbrake, and drive yourself to a railroad crossing. You will park your car on the rail tracks, turn the ignition off, and wait for the incoming train. You will play a worn cassette with songs by Tracy Chapman, Gloria Stephan, and, of course, Whitney Houston. Tracy Chapman will speak to you with her song, *Give Me One Reason*. You will agree with her. So simple. Give me a reason, a sign. Tap your lap. Snap your fingers. I'll be crawling up your English legs in a jiff. Seriously, honey. Can you hear yourself? And when Gloria Estefan sings *Don't Wanna Lose You*, your anthem of the day, you will nod in agreement like you are in a couples therapy session, promising the counselor you'll change your evil ways. Living, you will reason, is for those who are loved, and because you are not, you decide that this living gig is not for you. You will breathe in, hold your breath, and drink the rest of the bottle at once, determined to stay there until you see or imagine the train coming at you. And you will stay there stuck on the edges of reality, hearing the train squeal, or maybe it's not the train but your daughter squealing with delight because when you are the tickling monster, you are the funniest mommy ever. And the train will whistle, or maybe it's not the train but the memories of the day you taught your daughter to whistle and the delightful squealing that ensued. And amid this absurd moment, at that hazy intersection of panic and hope, you will feel her tiny hands on your cheek: Mommy, don't cry, she had said to you one night in the dark. And it will dawn on you that this tiny person had been awake in the middle of the night, irrevocably strapped to your sadness and bearing witness to the destruction of the only person she had in the world. And the thought of her will awaken something in you close to rapture, to faith, to the divine. That day while you waited for a train that never came, your daughter will become your goddess, beacon, and compass. The only Trinity you will ever need.

Here's the thing, honey. You will survive the carnage all by yourself. You will swim ashore without a therapist holding your hand through the process, without pills or spiritual retreats, without a support group to give you collective hugs or tap your back. You won't tell your family. You will get out of this mess on your own. You will leave him behind. Not because you are tough, but because you are intelligent enough to realize there is nothing in that relationship worth fighting for. You will leave the oil industry. Not because you are not smart enough, but because you understand that spending your life making money for a multinational that treats you like a small-town peddler is not a life but a sentence. You will leave Colombia because raising a little girl in the middle of a damn drug war is infanticide, and you can't afford to lose her to a culture consumed by street violence. You will finally understand that if a mess raises a mess, you will start a fatal cycle. But you won't. You will eventually get it. Clumsily. Unsteadily. But you will get it.

You will move to a faraway country where the Inuit have one hundred names for snow. You will quit smoking and drinking. You will become a Buddhist. You will practice Tai Chi and teach your daughter to ride a bike and dance merengue. You will learn English and go back to school to graduate top of the class despite being the only foreigner in the classroom. When you are given the summa cum laude sash at the graduation ceremony, you won't understand how momentous the event is. You will become a decent anthropologist. You will see the world. You will sit in the Arabian desert with your ten-year-old daughter as you explain the blood between her legs. You will teach her to shave her underarms and the importance of deodorant. Together you will go shopping for training bras, and later for the grown-up stuff. One African migration season will catch the both of you standing atop a ridge, holding hands, as you watch the wildebeest trample each other as they cross the Zambezi River. The same river will flip your raft over at a rapid named Oblivion, and as you flail your arms under the water and look desperately for your daughter, you will curse yourself for that day on the railway crossing. But she will think this is fun, and she will be riding the eddy in your direction, waving her arms in the air, Hi, Mom, and you'll hope she can swim this unburdened, this freely through the rapids of life coming her way as a woman.

You will start dancing and rediscover your body through kinetics. You will find that you are not too skinny, your nose is not too big, your teeth are not too crooked, and your hair is not too frizzy. You will accept the stretch marks on your tummy as a badge of honor for having brought a human being into the world and will learn to appreciate your flat chest and hips because, hey, at least they won't sag when you hit fifty. You will learn to look at yourself in the mirror and walk away with a smile and a nod.

Go ahead, get into the damn limo, sweetheart. Have it your way; just don't beat yourself up over the imminent onslaught. You will never get back these two years of your life, your very own dark ages. Know that chaos is not self-sustainable; it rearranges itself into manageable chunks of pedestrian life. Then, when you think life is hunky-dory, chaos will strike again, and your existence will be a continuous gestalt moment. I promise you, that's the best we can hope for. Your ordinary life will be filled with extraordinary moments, and by extraordinary, I don't necessarily mean beautiful. I mean finding the love of your life, losing him, getting him back. Nearly losing your daughter before she turns fifteen, driving her away to college, picking her up after she drops out, helping her find her way again, the blind leading the blind, wait another ten years before you get her back. All the while, she will make many mistakes. Not as bad as yours, although it will feel that way just because you are her mom. You will watch her fall in love many times, many false alarms, until one day, something clicks, she meets Miguel, and you will walk her down the aisle, convinced that he is the best thing that could happen to her. And he will be.

You will get into graduate school, and you will excel at it. You will meet a group of Indian maids working abroad, where they live a slave-like existence, and you will find your voice through their muted plight. Your dissertation will become an essay, and this essay a book, then two, then three, then many essays, and your life will be, for the first time, filled with a noble purpose: to work with and for other women, to bear witness to their strident falls as well as the rowdy soars, and commit memory to the page. Other women will inhabit your life. Mexican undocumented women will reveal their losses and triumphs to you, and from them, you will learn the true meaning of the word sacrifice. Through their suffering and courage, these women will make you softer, file down your rough edges, and open your eyes to the kind of beauty you'll learn to see, not with your eyes, but your soul.

Almost thirty years after you get into the limo and say *I Do* at the We've Only Just Begun chapel, you will think of your twenty-six-year-old self, scratch your head, and wonder what the fuck happened to you. The picture of that young woman in her ivory corset, ready to implode as she walks out of the Caesar's Palace Hotel, will remain a mystery to you, like the Bermuda Triangle, Amelia Earhart's death, the Dancing Plague of 1518. Something that happened, but you can't explain.

Somewhere along these thirty years, you will lose your estranged father, then your mother. Your friend's words who told you that a woman stops being a little girl only when she becomes an orphan will ring true for the first time. You will discover that your siblings are the Stonehenge of your existence, immovable, their love for one another unyielding; your sisters will become your heroines and your brother your first knight in shining armor. Your siblings, their children, who will feel like your own, and your daughter will cement your life, root you down, and give you wings. And they'll have your back whether you want to stay put or fly. It won't make any difference. So unwavering their love for you will be.

It will be rough, sweetheart, but eventually, one day, at fifty-four, when you become the best version of yourself, you will sit on a yoga mat and think of yourself at twenty-six. The concept of Ahimsa, nonviolence, will come to you. It has taken you thirty years to realize that this cardinal virtue is not only about not committing a violent act toward others but, more importantly, not being violent toward yourself—in thought, word, and deed. Alas, it will be too late to teach your younger self this. So, bring your hands together, close your eyes, and say thank you, for gratitude and self-forgiveness are the best antidotes to sins of the past.

Biographical Note

Páramo is a Colombian anthropologist, writer, and women's rights advocate. Her manuscript *Unsent Letters to My Mother* won the Faulkner Society's best nonfiction award. Her book *My Mother's Funeral* was nominated for the Latino Books into Movies Award. She is also the author of *Looking for Esperanza*, winner of the Social Justice and Equity Award in Creative Non-fiction; Nautilus Silver Award in the conscious media category; Best Women's Issues book at the International Latino Book Award; Best Social Studies book at the International Publishers' Awards; silver medal at the Book of the Year Award, BOYA, and was listed as one of the top ten best books by Latino authors.

Páramo writes from Medellín, Colombia.

9 781636 281841